The WORLD'S WORST

The WORLD'S WORST

A GUIDE TO *THE MOST*

DISGUSTING

HIDEOUS

Inept, and Dangerous People, Places, and

THINGS ON EARTH

Mark Frauenfelder

CHRONICLE BOOKS

SAN FRANCISCO

Library of Congress Cataloging-in-Publication Data available.

0-8118-4606-7

Printed in Canada.
Designed by Tim Belonax
Typeset in Bryant, Belizio, and Berthold Akzidenz Grotesk

Distributed in Canada by Raincoast Books
9050 Shaughnessy Street
Vancouver, British Columbia V6P 6E5

10 9 8 7 6 5 4 3 2 1

Chronicle Books LLC
85 Second Street
San Francisco, California 94105
www.chroniclebooks.com

To Carla, Sarina, and Jane—
the most wonderful girls on Earth.

CONTENTS

INTRODUCTION

Bookstore shelves are lined with volumes dedicated to the finest things in the world: the most exquisite dining experiences, the greatest athletes, the most brilliant military strategists, the most powerful automobiles. These books make for fine reading and serve as fuel for the unrealizable fantasies of the masses.

While it is good and proper to bestow honor upon those individuals and items that shine at the top of the heap, the truth is that the really entertaining stuff is taking place well below. It's here, in the sleazy, slipshod muck at the bottom of the barrel, where you'll find attention-grabbing creatures driven by greed, desperation, sloppy thinking, sloth, or hatred, busily devoting themselves to the worst life has to offer. It's here in the murky dregs where you'll find toys that maim and kill their young owners, fast-food meals that harbor more than twice the recommended daily allowance of fat between their pillow-soft buns, plastic surgery addicts who look like monsters from an old sci-fi movie, cars that operate as if they were designed by sadists, food additives that cause projectile bowel movements, plants and animals hell-bent on inflicting misery on us, and bank presidents who comport themselves like bratty three-year-olds.

With rubber gloves unrolled up to my armpits, I've reached deep into the barrel of the worst things on Earth, dredging up the most odious and most obscene specimens found there for your amusement and edification.

Ladies and gentlemen: it doesn't get any worse than this.

LEAST
ADORABLE
PET

MIRACLE MIKE
THE HEADLESS CHICKEN

Exotic pets are often quite ugly—that's part of the fun in having one. Their owners think it's neat to keep repulsive animals such as tarantulas, snakes, and hissing cockroaches. But such unadorable creatures are like cuddly teddy bears compared to Miracle Mike, the celebrated headless chicken of Fruita, Colorado.

Once upon a time, way back in 1945, Mike was but another unnamed rooster, just one of many chickens living on Lloyd and Clara Olsen's farm and destined for the refrigerated section of the grocery store. On September 10, Mr. Olsen selected several chickens for the chopping block. As usual after decapitation, each chicken scrambled and scratched for a moment by reflex. One rooster, however, kept running around the yard, as if it hadn't realized its head was sitting on the ground.

The next morning, the headless chicken was still proudly strutting around as if nothing had happened. Surprised and curious, the Olsens began feeding it, dripping a gruel of crushed grain and water down its throat, to see how long it could survive. And the rooster thrived—as much as it could without a head—climbing onto perches, making gurgling noises in an attempt to crow, and futilely attempting to preen its feathers with its phantom head.

Word about the headless rooster spread quickly through town and caught the attention of a local promoter named Hope Wade, who dubbed him "Miracle Mike" and sent him and the Olsens on the road. For 25 cents, people could enter a tent to see Miracle Mike in action, and peer into a liquid-filled jar containing the preserved remains of Mike's head. (Actually, it was the head of another chicken—the Olsens' cat had eaten Mike's real head.) Mike was a big hit, raking in $4,500 a month (more than $44,000 in today's money).

Soon, envious Fruitans began chopping off the heads of their own chickens with renewed enthusiasm, hoping to get another Mike—but no one was able to repeat the lucky mistake made by Olsen. He had delivered a blow that left enough of Mike's brain stem intact to allow it to function almost normally.

Unfortunately, Mike's second chance at life came to an end in March 1947. Because of his condition, Mike needed to have his throat cleared regularly with a syringe to prevent him from choking on his own mucus. But one fateful night, in a Phoenix, Arizona, hotel room, the sound of Miracle Mike's frantic rasping awakened the Olsens. The couple suddenly realized that they had left Mike's syringe back at the carnival, and they watched helplessly as the poor animal breathed his last breath, 18 months after having his head chopped off.

MOST
DISGUSTING
BEHAVIOR ON A
PLANE

GERARD B. FINNERAN

In a global culture that increasingly worships the ability to make money and wield power, chief executive officers have joined the media-created celebrity firmament. Fully aware of their exalted status, many CEOs expect mere mortals to bow down before them and to satisfy any capricious whims that may strike their fancy. If the demands aren't satisfied, the resulting temper tantrum can be very ugly.

How ugly? Take the case of Gerard B. Finneran. In 1995 Finneran, the 58-year-old head of an investment-banking firm, was seated in the first-class cabin on a United Airlines flight from Buenos Aires to New York. Taking advantage of the free liquor being served in that section of the plane, Finneran proceeded to get very, very drunk. After a concerned flight attendant refused to give him another glass of wine, Finneran took charge of the situation and began serving himself drinks from the beverage cart. When informed that it was against regulations for passengers to get their own drinks, an infuriated Finneran told the flight attendant that he was going to "bust [his] ass."

Threatening the crew failed to achieve Finneran's desired result, so he resorted to plan B: going berserk, terrifying passengers, knocking over crew members, and then grabbing drinks and pouring them over his body. He topped off the show with an educational demonstration of primate dominance, by clambering onto the beverage cart that had been placed offlimits to him and evacuating his bowels on it, using the first-class linen napkins (and his fingers) to wipe his hindquarters. According to the criminal complaint filed against him, this captain of industry then proceeded to clean his fingers by walking up and down the aisle, "track[ing] feces throughout the aircraft."

In court, Finneran pleaded guilty as charged, but his legal team claimed that the entire incident was a misunderstanding. Their client, they explained, had contracted a severe case of traveler's diarrhea, but couldn't use the first-class lavatories because they had been barricaded by assistants to the president of Portugal, who was also on the flight. In this situation, they argued, what choice did Finneran have but to defecate on the beverage cart?

The judge didn't buy it. Finneran was sentenced to 300 hours of community service and presented with a cleaning bill for $50,000. "I promise, Your Honor," Finneran told him, "you will never hear of me doing anything like this again."

MOST ROTTEN CHEESE

CASU MARZU

Even though cheese is pretty disgusting when you think about what it actually is, most cultures enjoy eating the coagulated mammary secretions of hoofed animals. Even blue cheese (which is little more than moldy fat) is considered good eating by many people. But when it comes to cheese infested by maggots, most folks draw the line.

Not the residents of Sardinia. They go for *casu marzu*, a festering pile of rotten pecorino cheese teeming with squirming fly larvae. Stashed away in cupboards and under counters at open-air markets due to its contraband status, *casu marzu* is a brown-colored cheese in which flies have been permitted —even encouraged—to deposit eggs. When the thousands of eggs hatch, the maggots eat the cheese and then release an enzyme, triggering a fermentation process that causes the fat in the cheese to putrefy. By the time the cheese is ready to be consumed, it's a gluey mass that creates a burning sensation in the mouth.

Because the still-living maggots will attempt to leap into the cheese eater's eyes, conventional wisdom dictates that you cover the cheese with your hand when you raise a piece to your lips. Squeamish *casu marzu* gourmands who don't want to ingest live maggots can first place the cheese in a paper bag and seal it. When the maggots become starved for oxygen, they jump out of the cheese and writhe in the bag, making a pitter-patter sound. When the sound subsides, that means the maggots are dead and the cheese is ready to eat.

A Sardinian health department official who was interviewed by the *Wall Street Journal* said anyone caught selling or serving the black market treat could be slapped with a heavy fine but admitted, "as a Sardinian and a man, let me tell you, I have never heard of anyone falling ill after eating this stuff. Sometimes, it tastes real good."

CREEPIEST TOY MAKER

HAROLD VON BRAUNHUT

Advertised for decades in comic books, the Amazing Live Sea-Monkeys are perhaps the greatest marketing scam ever perpetrated on children, with the possible exception of another phony product, X-Ray Spex. The see-through glasses are made from feathers sandwiched between pieces of cardboard with holes in them. Anyone who has ever bought a pair, hoping to see under people's clothes, has quickly come to the realization "So this is how a sucker sees the world."

An Amazing Live Sea-Monkey is not a primate. It's a brine shrimp—a translucent, nearly microscopic arthropod that doesn't originate from the sea and resembles a monkey only to the degree that a paper clip resembles the International Space Station.

Is it any wonder that both Sea-Monkeys and X-Ray Spex were created by the same man? His name was Harold von Braunhut, and he was not only a mechanical genius with 193 patents under his belt, he was also one of the slickest hucksters in the annals of merchandising. His Sea-Monkey brainchild was conceived in 1957 and brought to fruition in 1960. To depict the lowly brine shrimp as a jovial, pink-colored simian with a natural crown must go down as one of the world's greatest examples of false advertising. But even better than this wildly inaccurate and deceptive depiction of the creatures, however, is the copy von Braunhut wrote for the Sea-Monkeys' ubiquitous comic book advertisements: "In only five minutes you will actually hatch a whole tumbling, playful, happy troupe of Sea-Monkeys that are even more fun than a zoo full of chattering, howling jungle monkeys!"

Von Braunhut sold millions of dollars of his "fantastic underwater buffoons" to millions of soon-to-be-disappointed children who were expecting to see the "inanimate handful of glittering crystals which contain the secret of life" transform itself into a dancing school of "frolicsome pets" that "love attention!"

If von Braunhut were guilty of nothing more than stealing children's allowances, he might be forgiven. It was, after all, a small price to pay to learn the meaning of *caveat emptor* through firsthand experience.

Unfortunately, von Braunhut's transgressions don't end there. In the late 1980s, reports of the Sea-Monkey inventor's ties with white supremacist groups began to surface. An Aryan Nations fundraising letter stated that the manufacturer of a self-defense weapon called the Kiyoga Agent M5 was donating a portion of sales to Aryan Nations founder Richard Butler. Von Braunhut was the inventor of the weapon (a sort of telescoping metal whip, which he described as the weapon to buy "if you need a gun but can't get a license"). When the Spokane, Washington, *Spokesman-Review* interviewed Butler, he affirmed that von Braunhut was a friend and "member of the Aryan race who has supported us quite a few years." In 1988 the *Washington Post* picked up the story, reporting that von Braunhut regularly attended annual Aryan Nations World

Congress meetings, self-published an anti-Zionist newsletter, and once bought firearms for an Ohio branch of the Ku Klux Klan. A person who'd done business with von Braunhut told the paper that the inventor had once told him, "Hitler wasn't a bad guy. He just received bad press."

The strangest part of the incredibly strange life of this neo-Nazi Sea-Monkey magnate is that he was *Jewish,* born Harold Nathan Braunhut in Memphis on March 31, 1926. His being Jewish didn't seem to be a problem for the Aryan Nations or other white supremacist groups he gave money to.

When he died on November 28, 2003, at the age of 77, von Braunhut was reportedly perfecting his next two inventions: a pet lobster and an instant frog.

MOST DISAGREEABLE FOOD ADDITIVE

I n 1996 fried-food lovers around the world could not have been blamed for dropping to their knees and weeping with unashamed joy. For that was the year Procter & Gamble announced it had invented Olestra, a new kind of fat with zero (zero!) artery-clogging calories. It was a *miracle.*

How could such a thing be possible? Procter & Gamble's consumer information revealed precious little detail about the company's patented and closely guarded method for making the substance. It stated only that the process starts with "a vegetable oil, like soybean or cottonseed, and ordinary table sugar." Next, the oils and sugar were "processed in a whole new way" that "reduces their caloric value while retaining the creamy 'mouth-feel' of fat." This "whole new way" of combining sugar and fat formed a giant synthetic molecule, the likes of which has never appeared in nature.

Olestra (which Procter & Gamble calls "Olean" when used in food products) is free of calories because, unlike ordinary fat, it is unrecognizable to your body's digestive system. The enzymes in your intestines take one look at Olestra and say, "Whatever this stuff is, it's not my job," and allow it to pass through your system untouched.

This exit is where Olestra's problems begin. When products containing Olestra appeared on store shelves in 1998, potato chip junkies hoping for a free ride were taken aback—if only for a moment—to see product packages emblazoned with federal Food and Drug Administration–mandated labels warning that Olestra could cause "abdominal cramping" and "loose stools." As part of the Olestra approval process, the FDA had conducted a Fecal Parameters Study, in which lucky scientists had been given the task to examine the composition of olestra-eaters' stool samples. Evidence of the digestive consequences warranted the label.

But some advocacy groups didn't think the labels went far enough in warning consumers of the potentially "explosive" effects of the fake fat. According to the Center for Science in the Public Interest, more than 20,000 complaints about Olestra-induced gastrointestinal discomfort have been submitted to the FDA, either directly to the agency or via CSPI, since the faux fat came on the market.

In 2002 a CSPI press release described its report to the FDA as "brimming with grisly reports of diarrhea, fecal incontinence, cramping, bleeding, and yellow-orange oil in toilet bowls and in underwear." According to the CSPI, one man "required emergency room treatment after complaining of 'violent' vomiting and 'projectile' bowel movements after eating Wow! potato chips."

In December 1999, Procter & Gamble filed a petition with the FDA to have the warning labels removed from products containing Olestra. Due in no small part to the appetite-reducing effect of the label, sales of Olestra, which started out with a bang at $400 million in 1998, had plummeted to half that by 2000. In August 2003, the FDA granted the request after concluding, "Olestra caused only infrequent, mild gastrointestinal effects." The CSPI, however, stands by its findings. Executive Director Michael F. Jacobson warned that the decision "will condemn many more people to the diarrhea and cramps that Olestra too often causes."

SADDEST
FATE
FOR AN
ISLAND
NATION

THE DEMISE OF NAURU

Most people have never heard of Nauru. The world's smallest independent republic, Nauru is an eight-square-mile island that lies halfway between Hawaii and New Zealand and has a population of around 12,000. One hundred years ago, Nauru was a sparkling emerald of dense tropical forests surrounded by blue water, much like the thousands of other islands scattered across Polynesia. Today, 90 percent of Nauru resembles a moonscape, with only a thin strip of greenery around its perimeter. What happened? It was the Nauruans' good and then very bad luck to be living on one of the only islands in the South Pacific to be made almost entirely of high-grade phosphate, an important fertilizer ingredient—the result of migratory sea birds having used the atoll as a rest stop for eons.

When a German-British consortium found out about the phosphate in the early twentieth century, it moved in with steam shovels and started scooping away the island's interior, compensating native landowners a half penny for each ton of phosphate they hauled away. By the time Nauru won its independence in 1968, an estimated two-thirds of its surface had been mined. With independence came a *much* better return on the phosphate—the island's only real exportable asset—so the mining continued unabated. Now that the money was good, why turn back? As the *Economist* reported, "For a brief, heady moment in the 1970s, Nauruans were, astonishingly, among the richest people on earth." They enjoyed tax-free lives filled with wonderful perks, and work was strictly optional.

Then, two bad things happened: First, the Nauruans lost their fortune to con artists, who swindled them with bogus money-market schemes and, most notably, a crazy investment in a theatrical musical about the life of Leonardo da Vinci (*Leonardo: A Portrait of Love*) that lost millions of dollars. Second, Nauru essentially ran out of Nauru. The island had literally been hauled away, shipload by shipload. What little phosphate remains is too expensive to extract, so most foreign mining companies have picked up their equipment and left. Today Nauru is on the verge of bankruptcy and limps along by selling passports, providing unreported banking services (to such clients as the Russian Mafia, which has laundered an estimated $70 billion there), and presenting itself as a miserable holding and detention camp for Australian-bound refugees.

In the fall of 2004, Nauru found itself unable to continue financing its massive debt and was forced to relinquish the property portfolio it had acqured in the boom days and put it up as collateral, including several hotels in

Sydney and Melbourne and a range of shopping centers. Nauru's health minister announced that the government was "basically broke,' while the island's finance minister opined that the asylum seekers being held in Nauru's Australian-subsidized detention camp were more fortunate than the island's own residents. "The facilities they provide in those centers are better than we can provide for our own people."

To make matters worse, Nauruans rank among the most obese people on the planet, thanks to their need to import preserved food (even fresh water has to be shipped in). Over 50 percent of the population has diabetes, and the life expectancy is 20 years less than that of people living in nearby developed countries.

As if all of that weren't enough, Nauru itself may one day cease to exist. Evidence suggests that ocean levels are rising and that eventually the Nauruans may have to evacuate. Then, Nauru will be nothing but a bad memory.

WORST-SMELLING FLOWER

CORPSE BLOSSOM

The *Amorphophallus titanium* blooms only a few times during its 40-year life, but when it does, it alerts everyone within sniffing range. Commonly known as the corpse flower, *Amorphophallus titanium* (Latin for "giant shapeless penis") generates a nauseous cocktail of cadaverene and putrescine—by-products of decomposing flesh—along with a host of other malodorous sulfurous compounds. Using the starch in its 150-pound tuberous root for fuel, the plant heats up to 90°F to vaporize its repulsive-smelling volatile oils. The reek of rotting animal flesh is so strong that a person a half mile away can detect it.

Native to the Sumatran jungles of Indonesia, where it's called *bunga bangkai*, the 12-foot corpse flower, which erupts on a 20-foot stem, exudes its sickening scent of death in order to lure in flesh flies, sweat bees, dung beetles, and other assorted carrion-eating insects, which the plant relies on for pollination. They're not the most alluring creatures to have a one-night stand with, but you can't blame hummingbirds and honeybees for preferring to mingle with orange blossoms instead.

A few days after pollination, the corpse flower's blossom (which resembles an enormous, dead-flesh-colored banana in a fancy skirt) collapses, and the tuber begins saving up its energy to repeat the act in a decade or so. For dung beetles, that's a long time to wait. For everyone else who's had to smell a corpse flower, it's not nearly long enough.

MOST
DISGUSTING
FRUIT

DURIAN

Durian is the kind of crop the monster from *Alien* would grow in her backyard. Weighing as much as 10 pounds, this Southeast Asian fruit has a hard greenish shell studded with hard spikes, like some kind of living medieval weapon. Growing at the top of 40-foot-tall trees, durian fruits have been known to drop from their branches and kill people below.

It takes a mighty thwack of a machete to persuade a durian to yield its cache of grayish yellow sluglike pods. With an odor somewhere between sweetened garlic and pig manure, the fruit's stench is so overpowering that it can be smelled through a car's closed trunk.

Despite the fact that—or more likely, because—durian is so foul, it's considered a delicacy by millions of people. People love it or hate it, there is no in-between. Those who adore it as the "King of Fruit" in its native Indonesia, Malaysia, and especially

Thailand (which dominates the export market) are willing to fork over what amounts to a month's salary for a prime specimen. In Singapore alone, $30 million worth of the fetid fruit slithers down gullets of fearless gourmands each year. The governments of several Asian countries forbid people from bringing durian onto any type of public transportation. Most hotels have a ban on the fruit, and rental car agencies issue fines for cars that are returned smelling of it.

Many visitors to these countries are tempted to try durian. Here are some reports published on the Internet:

"I nearly vomited from the smell alone. I would describe it as a cross between dirty diapers and propane."

"It's like eating ice cream in a sewer."

"It really does smell like decaying flesh combined with rotting eggs."

"It was similar to eating a cheesecake covered with a layer of feces."

"That is the single most disgusting thing I've ever experienced in my life; get it out of my face."

The civet cat, common in Southeast Asia (and which plays a starring role in the Most Disgusting Beverage, see page 47), is also a fan of durian, and some attribute the cat's tastiness to its feeding on the fruit.

LEAST
HEALTHY
DIET

→

BREATHARIANISM

f you're a vegetarian, you might feel morally superior to meat eaters. If you're a vegan, eschewing all animal products, you most likely turn up your nose at weak-willed vegetarians who succumb to cheese. Fruitarians, who consume only fruit, nuts, and seeds, are haughtier still. But at the very top of the holier-than-thou diet list are breatharians, who claim to subsist on nothing but air and light. They don't even need to drink water.

The most well-known advocate of breatharianism is Jasmuheen (née Ellen Greve), a former businesswoman from Australia who claims she hasn't eaten any real food since 1993. (Her last meal was a falafel ball.) In her book *Living on Light, the Source of Nourishment for the New Millennium*, Jasmuheen writes about how "Ascended Masters" speak to her via cosmic telepathy and how she is able to draw upon invisible "pranic energy" for her sustenance. She boasts of having more than 6,000 followers. Because she doesn't eat, she says, she excretes only "rabbit-type droppings every three weeks."

Skeptics abound. On more than one occasion, reporters have discovered that Jasmuheen's house has food in it. She explains that the food is actually for her husband, Jess

Ferguson, a vegan (as well as a convicted felon who served time for fraud). In one instance, an Australian journalist who was on the same flight as Jasmuheen was surprised to see an airline attendant ask the cult leader to confirm that she'd ordered a vegetarian meal. After initially denying that she had, she said, "Yes, I did, but I won't be eating it." (Perhaps she only wanted to save the vegetables from being eaten.)

In a 1997 interview with the Australian Broadcasting Corporation, a reporter asked Jasmuheen if she'd eaten anything at all since starting her diet. She replied, "Maybe a few cups of tea and a glass of water, but now and then if I feel a bit bored and I want some flavor, then I will have a mouthful of whatever it is I'm wanting the flavor of. So it might be a piece of chocolate or it might be a mouthful of a cheesecake or something like that."

The reporter then asked her if she'd be willing to take a blood test to back up her claim that her DNA was changing shape from 2 strands to 12, in order to absorb more hydrogen. Jasmuheen answered, "Oh that depends. What I'd rather do is people go and have a look at the work of the Dalai Lama for example. Like in 1991—" The reporter interrupted her, asking her again why she wouldn't take the blood test, especially since the Australian Skeptics organization was offering her $30,000 if she could prove her DNA had changed. She said, "For blood test for DNA, I don't know. I'd have to really think about that one. I don't know what the relevance for it is."

In 1999 Jasmuheen agreed to undergo a challenge issued by *60 Minutes* in Australia. She was confined to a hotel room and placed under a doctor's care. When she showed signs of high blood pressure, dehydration, and stress after only two days, she blamed it on air pollution. The show's producers moved her to a mountain retreat, where she said the air was much better. But after another two days, it was clear that she was ill: her speech was slow, her pupils were dilated, her pulse almost double. The doctor said Jasmuheen was so dehydrated that her kidneys were in danger of being damaged. *60 Minutes* called off the experiment. Jasmuheen said it was the show's fault for putting her in a hotel next to a busy road at the beginning.

To date, three of Jasmuheen's followers have starved to death. One of them, 53-year-old Lani Morris of Melbourne, was seven days into the breatharian diet when she lost the ability to speak and the use of one arm. When Morris died three days later, Jasmuheen suggested that the woman was "not coming from a place of integrity and did not have the right motivation."

MOST
DISGUSTING
BEVERAGE

KOPI LUWAK

I n industrialized nations, where almost everything we drink comes out of a can, bottle, or carton, even something as innocuous as tap water is considered suspect enough to be a last-resort thirst quencher. Many Westerners would rather risk kidney failure from dehydration than imbibe a glass of *khoona*, an Afghan tribal wedding-ceremony drink made of still-warm bull semen, or the African Masai concoction of cow's blood and milk curdled in cow urine.

But the title of world's worst drink must be awarded to *kopi luwak*, an Asian beverage brewed from partially digested coffee beans that have been excreted from the anus of the civet cat, a furry black-and-white animal that looks like a weasel. (The civet also plays a supporting role in the story of the Most Disgusting Fruit, the durian—see page 40.)

Never mind that civet cats are suspected to be one of the main carriers of the deadly SARS virus in Asia, *kopi luwak* fans can't get enough of the stuff and are willing to pay up to $150 per pound for the fecally fortified beans, making this not only the most repulsive drink on the planet, but also one of the most expensive.

Why the demand for civet-bean coffee? Aficionados say the cats eat only the choicest beans, and their stomach acids impart a special flavor and aroma to the beans unmatched by standard processes. Surprisingly, many coffee connoisseurs agree. Despite *kopi luwak*'s distasteful origins, it apparently makes a delicious cup of joe.

"The aroma was rich and strong," wrote food critic Chris Rubin of his experience with *kopi luwak*, "and the coffee was incredibly full bodied, almost syrupy. It was thick, with a hint of chocolate, and lingered on the tongue with a long, clean aftertaste." He described *kopi luwak* as "one of the best cups I've ever had."

Besides the thick and syrupy part, you probably can't say the same thing for *khoona*.

WORST
MOLASSES-
RELATED
DISASTER

GREAT BOSTON FLOOD OF 1919

You'd be hard-pressed to find a more innocuous substance in your kitchen than molasses. Who would ever
suspect that this thick, dark, and homey sweetener could
also be a terrifying, fast-moving killer?

Newspaper accounts report that January 15, 1919—the day
of the Great Molasses Flood of Boston, Massachusetts—began
like any other winter day in that city, except for one thing. The
weather was unusually warm, reaching 40°F by midmorning.
This was probably a welcome event for Bostonians, who had
suffered through frigid 2°F temperatures the day before. But
little did anyone guess what havoc this extreme temperature
swing would soon wreak.

The sudden rise in temperature compromised the structural integrity of a 50-foot-tall steel tank filled with 2,320,000
gallons of molasses. Owned and maintained by the U.S.
Alcohol Company, the tank had been filled to capacity in
order to make as much hooch as possible before the alcohol

prohibition law kicked in. Just after noon on the 15th, the lunchtime crowd in the vicinity of the tank (located on the waterfront in Boston's densely populated North End) heard a thunderous explosion, immediately followed by what must have been the weirdest thing they had ever seen in their lives: a 25-foot-high wall of syrup washing toward them through the streets at 30 miles per hour. For 21 of these unfortunate witnesses, it would be the last thing they would ever see. Some were engulfed and smothered in the dark goo like prehistoric insects trapped in amber. Others were killed when the molasses ripped buildings from their foundations, or simply reduced them to rubble. Another 150 people were injured.

The *New York Times* of January 16, 1919, reported that a section of the tank wall fell on a nearby firehouse, crushing the building and three firemen inside. Freight cars were smashed; a warehouse yard was leveled. Horses became hopelessly mired in the goo and were shot. Rescue teams had a difficult time slogging through the thick syrup, which rose several feet high throughout the neighborhood.

Because the molasses stuck to everything it touched, the cleanup took several years and millions of dollars. Even so, residents reported that molasses would seep up from the ground on hot days as many as 30 years after the flood. And to this day, sharp-nosed Bostonians swear they can smell the stuff when the temperature rises.

WEIRDEST
QUACK
MEDICINE
SIDE EFFECT

TURNING BLUE

The best thing you can hope for from a quack medicine is that nothing bad happens to you. The worst thing is you die. The weirdest thing is you turn blue.

In the early part of the twentieth century, medicines containing microscopic silver particles were sold as a way to cure infections. They were popular as nose drops. In the grim era before antibiotics, "colloidal silver" solutions were one of the only ways to treat infections. While it's true that microscopic silver particles have some germ-killing properties, much more effective and safer drugs have since replaced them.

Unfortunately, quick-buck hucksters push colloidal silver on the Internet in the same way that traveling medicine-show scam artists sold bogus remedies out of horse-drawn wagons in the nineteenth century. They claim that big drug companies and the government have conspired to suppress this miracle drug. They spend a lot of time explaining why their particular version of colloidal silver is the only kind that works. They claim that their nostrums successfully treat acne, AIDS, allergies, appendicitis, arthritis, athlete's foot, bites, bladder infections, blood parasites, boils, bronchitis, burns, cancer, candida, chronic fatigue syndrome, colitis, dandruff, diabetes, diphtheria, gonorrhea, hay fever, head lice, hepatitis, herpes, impetigo, leprosy, leukemia, Lyme disease, malaria, meningitis, pneumonia, rheumatism, ringworm, scarlet fever, shingles, ulcers, viruses, warts, and yeast infections, among hundreds of other maladies.

The only thing the hucksters don't claim colloidal silver can treat is argyria, an irreversible blue-gray skin condition *caused* by the ingestion of silver.

Argyria first shows up under the fingernails and around the mouth and nose, then spreads across the surface of the skin. The skin literally turns into a living photographic plate (some black-and-white photographs contain silver as the photosensitive material), becoming dark when exposed to light and chemicals in the body. Unfortunately, there's no way to "unexpose" the skin once it takes on this ghastly, corpselike color.

Not surprisingly, people with argyria say their condition draws a lot of unwanted attention. Strangers stare at them, and little children point in astonishment. In 1996 a woman named Rosemary told a Canadian reporter what it is like to have argyria. In 1953, when she was 11 years old, her doctor prescribed colloidal silver nose drops for her colds. At the age of 14, a pharmacist looked at her one day and said, "Why are you that color?" Soon after, it became obvious to everyone that Rosemary was ash gray. She stopped taking the drops, but the condition didn't clear up.

Insensitive idiots all over the world have confronted her in public: "In Spain, people on the street would yell at me that I was a terrible color," she told the reporter. "I speak Spanish and I learned to yell back. In Germany, people would bluntly ask what was wrong with my face." Seeking a solution, Rosemary underwent dermabrasion to get rid of the layer of stained skin, but it was only partially successful. Her face is now bluish gray with pink blotches.

As a public service, Rosemary publishes a Web site to warn people against taking colloidal silver. On it she writes that the only thing she recommends colloidal silver for is as "a gray skin dye...it is safe, effective, and permanent when used for that purpose."

In 2002, Montana's Libertarian candidate for the United States Senate, 63-year-old Stan Jones, became the best-known proponent of colloidal silver, his skin having turned blue from years of drinking home-brewed silver solution. Jones said he started drinking the silver elixir, which he made by placing silver wires in a glass of water and running electricity through them, because he was concerned that a Y2K catastrophe could result in an antibiotic shortage. On the campaign trail, Jones joked about his coloring. "People ask me if it's permanent and if I'm dead," he told reporters. "I tell them I'm practicing for Halloween." He has also said that he regrets only that he "overdosed" on the solution, and remains convinced of its curative properties. "Being alive is more important than turning purple," he said. He lost the election.

SCARIEST
CELEBRITY
PLASTIC
SURGERY

JOCELYNE WILDENSTEIN

As the world's aging population takes inventory of its lumps, bumps, and wrinkles, it is forking over an estimated $160 billion a year to have them surgically removed and carted away in medical waste containers. The number of cosmetic procedures such as nose jobs, liposuction, Botox injection, breast augmentation, collagen lip injection, chemical peels, microdermabrasion, eyelid surgery, and laser hair removal performed in the United States rose to 6.9 million in 2002, with similarly dramatic recent increases in Europe and Asia. And while millions of people elect to have cosmetic treatments every year, it's the celebrities and socialites, bathed in the wattage of flashbulbs, who consider plastic surgery as essential a component of their lifestyle as frequent trips to rehab and converting to an Eastern religion.

Unfortunately, some of them don't know when to quit. As inhuman as Michael Jackson may look, he's a plastic surgery amateur when it comes to New York socialite Jocelyne Wildenstein, a.k.a. the "Bride of Wildenstein," who spent millions of dollars to remake herself in the image of a jungle cat.

By this standard, Wildenstein's bizarrely protruding facial implants, double-sized lips, and severely slanted eyes can be considered something of a success. She is reportedly quite happy with the results, and has downplayed her plastic surgery as just another part of her "health regimen."

It was her husband, billionaire art dealer Alec Wildenstein's fondness for young women that convinced her to get her first operation (an eye tuck) when she was 31. The implants, carvings, and injections continued for decades, but unfortunately didn't do the trick. In 1997, when Jocelyne Wildenstein returned home early from a trip to the family's 66,000-acre ranch in Kenya, she caught her husband in bed with a teenage model. He responded by grabbing a gun and chasing her and her bodyguards out of the house. He then took the girl for a dip in the pool, where he was later arrested.

After a lengthy public divorce trial, a judge awarded Jocelyne a $160,000 monthly alimony, but said she must pay for all future plastic surgery procedures herself. Maybe she should have gotten herself a better lawyer.

MOST
LETHAL
CLUTTER

THE COLLYER BROTHERS

At 10 a.m., on March 21, 1947, police officers of the 122nd Street police station in New York City were dispatched to a house on the corner of Fifth Avenue and 128th Street in Harlem. A mysterious call had come in an hour earlier to report a body inside.

When the officers tried to enter the decrepit four-story brownstone mansion, they couldn't get in. The door was locked. There was no doorbell, and the windows had been boarded up. They broke down the door but found their path barricaded from floor to ceiling by junk, including stacks of newspapers, cardboard boxes, gardening tools, folding chairs and beds, wooden chests, oil paintings, canvas bags, cornets, bugles, statues, and parts from a sewing machine and a wine press.

The police used a ladder to enter a window on the second story. They found a similarly bewildering load of debris blocking their way. Slowly they began picking through the dense farrago, which extended throughout the house, until they found a narrow path winding through the once-magnificent mansion. After several hours of combing through a dense nest of garden rakes, wire coils, umbrellas, folded paper bags, and bicycle parts, they found the body of Homer Collyer. The 66-year-old man had long gray hair and was dressed in a tattered bathrobe. The coroner's report concluded that Homer, blind and bedridden, hadn't eaten in several days, and had died of a heart attack. Not much was known about him. Neighbors said he had a brother, Langley, who took care of him, but nobody knew where he was.

Homer had been born in 1881, his brother six years later. They came from a well-to-do family—their father was a successful doctor—and both brothers attended Columbia University. Homer earned a law degree and went on to become a lawyer; Langley studied engineering and chemistry, but never worked, preferring to invent gadgets and dabble in music. Both parents had died by 1929, and the brothers stayed on in the mansion. Eventually they disconnected their phone, gas, and water. Langley collected their water from a park four blocks away. When Homer had a stroke in 1933, losing his eyesight and mobility, Langley prescribed a diet consisting of 100 oranges per week, plus plenty of black bread and peanut butter, in an attempt to cure him.

It took workers 18 days to clear the brothers' collection of clutter from the house. They found 14 grand pianos, a horse-drawn carriage, two organs, a Model T chassis, an X-ray machine, several glass jars containing human organs, 14,000 books, a car engine, dressmaker's dummies, rifles, shotguns, swords, toys, musical instruments, a 100-foot-long rolled-up rug and 13 Oriental rugs, 13 mantel clocks, and hundreds of gramophone records. And that's just for starters.

About 136 tons later, they also found Langley. His body was buried under a pile of newspapers and luggage, which he had apparently set as a booby trap to foil would-be intruders. Langley was wearing four pairs of pants, three jackets, a bathrobe, and an onion sack safety-pinned around his neck. The sack had apparently snagged on the trap's trigger. He wasn't wearing underwear or socks. He had died just eight feet away from Homer, who died several days later, according to the autopsy reports.

Being well-known eccentrics, the Collyers were occasionally featured in tabloid newspaper stories in the late 1930s. In one interview, Langley was asked why he kept tons of newspapers dating back 30 years. He said he was saving them for Homer, "so that when he regains his sight he can catch up on the news."

CRUELEST FOOD PREPARATION

While certain cultures venerate the animals that they eat, most people try not to think of the death of the animal they are consuming. It's not much of an appetite booster. Imagine a restaurant that marched cattle into the dining area, so patrons could see them receive a stunning blow on the forehead from a concussion gun, before they were taken away to be strung up, skinned, and eviscerated. "At least the animal didn't suffer," you might say, as you carve into your filet mignon.

But some animals do suffer when people eat them. North Korea's leader, Kim Jong Il, is just one of many gourmands who enjoy sashimi carved from a live fish, and countless people have shucked oysters or tossed a squirming lobster into a pot of boiling water.

In most cases, the animal's demise is simply a side effect of the method of preparation. But there's a dish in Japan, called *dojo jigoku*, in which pain and suffering seem to be the main attraction. Dojo is an eel-like freshwater fish related to the carp. The name of the dish, which translates as "dojo hell," gives you an idea of the treatment the fish receive.

The recipe is simple: Place a pot of soup stock on a burner at the center of a dining table. Make sure everyone has a clear view of the pot. Set a block of cold tofu into the liquid, and pour in a dozen live baby dojo. Then turn on the burner and watch the fun. As the liquid heats up, the fish try to get away by burrowing into the cooler tofu. But of course, after just a few minutes in boiling stock, even the center of the tofu is piping hot, and the baby dojo are fully cooked.

To serve, remove the tofu to a decorative dish, slice, and serve like olive loaf.

WORST

GRUDGE

AGAINST

NATURE

TROY HURTUBISE

vs.

"THE OLD MAN"

When a wild animal attacks a human being, the psychic wounds are often worse than the actual bodily injury. While some people undergo psychotherapy to deal with such post-traumatic stress, a few Old Testament types seek revenge on the beast that hurt them by retaliating in kind. And of all the modern-day Captain Ahabs on Earth, none is more determined to settle the score than a Canadian scrap-metal dealer by the name of Troy Hurtubise.

In August 1984, at the age of 19, Hurtubise went camping alone near Humidity Creek in British Columbia. One afternoon after panning for gold, he discovered a giant grizzly bear in his camp. The bear ran over to him and knocked him in the dirt with a head-butt to the chest. Certain that he would die, Hurtubise decided to go out with a bang. He leaped to his feet and pulled out not one, but two, hunting knives (he carries as many as ten at a time) and, according to his own account of the incident in *Outside* magazine, told the bear, "Take what you want, but I'll take both of these knives and I'll shove them right up your ass." The bear, apparently getting the gist of Hurtubise's declaration, retreated into the woods, never to be seen again.

Because the bear that attacked him had gray chin hairs, Hurtubise dubbed it "the Old Man." In fact, Hurtubise now calls any grizzly "the Old Man." To him, they're all the same bear—the one that knocked him down.

Brooding over the incident, Hurtubise decided that he wanted to meet the Old Man once again, this time on more even terms. To do that, he began work on a suit of armor that could withstand the crushing blows and deadly bites of a grizzly bear. After six years, $100,000 scraped together from his personal income, and several versions of the suit, he felt he had finally designed a model that was ready for combat. The Mark IV consists of toughened rubber, chain mail, inflatable cushions, an arm-mounted canister of bear repellent, and a titanium-encased motorcycle helmet. The end result, which weighs 147 pounds, looks like a cross between a deep-sea diving suit and RoboCop.

While perfecting his bear-proof suit, Hurtubise attempted to test it on the black bears that forage through the garbage dumps at night near his house in North Bay, Ontario. He tried to raise the ire of the bears by charging at them, but they ran away from the queer biped. Later attempts to tussle with grizzlies in the wild (with a documentary film crew in tow) also failed to yield any takers.

But Hurtubise persisted, building new and improved versions of the bear-fighting suit. His latest, the Ursus Mark VII, features an exoskeleton of stainless steel, aluminum and titanium armor, an internal cooling system, a video screen, air bags, shock absorbers, and a robotic third arm.

In December 2001, Hurtubise stepped into a fenced-off enclosure in western Canada to face a nine-foot-tall, 1,290-pound Kodiak bear owned by an animal trainer. "This isn't going to be a wrestling match, but a controlled attack,"

Hurtubise told reporters. "I've waited 15 years for this. I've tested the suit against bullets, knives, arrows, trucks, logs, rocks, and cars to see if I could handle the power of a bear. And now I'll find out against the real thing and see if I can put my critics to rest." When bear and man squared off in the enclosure, the Kodiak kept its distance, warily studying the suited-up Hurtubise. After 10 minutes, it approached, coming within six inches.

"I could smell his breath through my helmet," Hurtubise reported. "When he was that close, I really got terrified and my heart was just pounding in my chest." At that point, the Kodiak's trainer, who could see the tremendous size and weight difference between the two, called off the event.

Today, Hurtubise claims he wants to encounter bears in order to test bear sprays and research the ursine behemoths from up close. "It's the science I'm interested in," he says.

Sure, it's the science.

MOST
GRUESOME
BUG BITE

Bad things can come in small packages. And one of the most horrible small packages is the brown recluse spider, found throughout the south-central United States. Normally the quarter-inch brown recluse (also known as the "fiddleback spider" because of the distinctive violinlike mark on its back) is a timid creature, preferring to while away its 10-year lifespan in woodpiles and dark corners. But when a brown recluse is disturbed, it bites. At first, victims often have no idea that they have been wounded by the creature's tiny jaws. But they soon find out.

In a few hours, the tiny droplet of venom, *sphingomyelinase D*, delivered in the spider's bite causes a small, reddened area resembling a mosquito bite. Unlike the localized itch centered on a mosquito bite, however, the entire limb on which the victim received the bite begins to itch; this is often followed by excruciating pain, fever, nausea, and bloody urine. Twenty-four hours after the attack, the general area around the bite swells, the redness spreads, and an ugly-looking white blister forms in the center. Around this time, the victim starts to freak out. But this is only the beginning of a horrific ordeal.

Joint pain, chills, nausea, and fever continue for the next couple of days as the skin around the wound begins to harden, as though the body were attempting to armor itself against further damage. Unfortunately, the toxin is already under the skin, doing its nasty work of dissolving cell membranes of the flesh surrounding the bite. The surface area around the lesion (now about two inches in diameter) takes on a characteristic red, white, and blue color scheme, as though in patriotic salute to the spider's national habitat.

From here, there are two paths: lucky, and not-so-lucky. If the victim is lucky, this is as bad as it ever gets—the wound heals, leaving only a patchy, sunken, bluish scar as a reminder to steer clear of the petulant arachnid. The not-so-lucky will find themselves suffering through the health-care equivalent of a Jerry Bruckheimer disaster movie playing out across their flesh. The bite erupts into what's called a *volcano lesion*—a deep, jagged-edged black hole oozing with gangrenous tissue. Victims who endure this fate usually end up in hospital beds with several tubes sticking out of them, as the wound grows to resemble a small pizza glued onto their body. In some cases, it's necessary to amputate the necrotizing limb to prevent the wound from spreading. In rare instances, the victim dies.

Perhaps the most frightening thing about this spider bite is the tendency for relapse. Some victims who appear fully cured will suddenly reexperience necrosis months or even years after the original symptoms have vanished. People so unlucky as to have been bitten must go through their lives wondering when the kiss of the brown recluse will resurface and start the cycle of horror all over again.

LOUSIEST-TASTING CIGARETTE

PREMIER

Tobacco companies aren't run by heartless moneygrubbers who don't care if you die from smoking. On the contrary, they're run by heartless moneygrubbers who want you to live so you keep buying their product. Case in point: look at the effort R.J. Reynolds put into developing and marketing a "smokeless" cigarette, which the company implied (but never stated directly) was a healthier alternative to regular cigarettes.

In 1988, after seven years of research and development, RJR introduced the Premier, a marvel of nicotine-delivery technology. Although Premier cigarettes looked like any other cancer stick, they were actually aluminum tubes filled with tobacco-flavored, nicotine-enhanced pellets. Unlike an ordinary cigarette, which burns tobacco to be inhaled as smoke, the Premier heated up the pellets, releasing their nicotine in the form of a smokeless vapor.

The Premier cigarette cost an estimated $800 million to develop and market, so you'd think (and RJR had certainly hoped) that the result would be tasty and simple to use. It was not. First of all, the Premier was so difficult to figure out that each package came with its own four-page instructional booklet. Smokers would have smoked a Marlboro just to relieve the stress from trying to light up the Premier's carbon element, which one analyst said "took a blowtorch" to ignite.

And those smokers who figured out how to successfully fire up a Premier had to suck so hard on it to get any flavor that RJR researchers called the phenomenon the "hernia effect." The reward for so much sucking? A taste that polite testers described as "charcoal." One lyrical tester said the aroma was "as if you'd just opened a grave on a warm day." More plain-speaking smokers said it "tastes like shit" and "smells like a fart."

Research by RJR claimed that smokers would have to smoke two or three packs before growing accustomed to the Premier's peculiarities, but in the real world, smokers tried one, flinched, and got rid of the rest of the pack by passing them out to curious friends. Four months after its debut, the Premier—one of the most colossal marketing blunders in history—was snuffed out for good.

MOST
EXCESSIVE
SOFT-DRINK
CONTAINER

THE BEAST

Until 1,000 years ago, people consumed less than a few pounds of sugar per year, mostly in fruit, occasionally in honey. By 1915, thanks to the introduction of carbonated soft drinks, people were ingesting between 15 and 20 pounds of sugar a year. Soda turned out to be an excellent sugar-delivery system—much better than other forms of sweet food, which require wearisome mastication. Colas can be poured down gullets without effort, goading pancreases into squeezing out gushers of brain-numbing insulin.

In 1975, when Coca Cola still came in 6-ounce bottles, North Americans consumed an average of 120 pounds of sugar a year. That's a lot of sugar, but not enough for the sugar and beverage manufacturers. In their quest to appease stockholders by selling more sugar water every year, marketers hatched the now-pervasive idea of "value," or "super," sizing—offering more of a product than a customer actually needs for a relatively low extra cost—and began selling their fizzy syrups in 20-ounce single-serving bottles. In 1999 per-capita sugar consumption zoomed to 170 *pounds a year* (much of it in the form of cheap high-fructose corn syrup), and it is still climbing. This is unfortunate, because high sugar intake is associated with a host of health problems, including diabetes, obesity, heart disease, and tooth decay.

With the 7-Eleven convenience stores chain's introduction of its 32-ounce Big Gulp in 1984, the floodgates of excessive soda consumption had truly been flung open. Customers were soon offered even more monstrous servings of fizzing, flavored corn syrup: the Super Big Gulp (44 ounces), the X-treme Gulp (52 ounces), and the supertanker of soft drinks, the Double Gulp (64 ounces—a half gallon of soda complete with 600 calories and 48 *teaspoons of sugar*).

With upwards of 25,000 stores located across the United States, Canada, Japan, Australia, Mexico, Taiwan, Singapore, the Philippines, the United Kingdom, Sweden, Denmark, South Korea, Thailand, Norway, Turkey, Malaysia, China, Singapore, and Guam, 7-Eleven sells 33 million gallons of soda a year.

Now, 7-Eleven may be one of the pioneers in supersizing and a global presence, but if you really want to imbibe the world's largest fountain drink, you'll have to travel to the United States and enter an AM/PM Minimart. Give the person behind the counter $2.49 and ask for "The Beast." You'll be rewarded with an *85-ounce* cup of soda—the equivalent of seven 12-ounce cans. If that's still not enough for you, don't despair: refills are just $1.29.

1964   2004

MADDEST MAD SCIENTIST

THE CIA'S DR. SIDNEY GOTTLIEB

On a warm autumn evening in Paris in 1952, a 25-year-old, up-and-coming American artist named Stanley Glickman was enjoying a coffee at his favorite haunt, the Café Dome in Montparnasse. Perhaps he spent the moment thinking of his Canadian girlfriend who was touring Europe at the time, or of the painting he'd completed that was hanging in New York's Metropolitan Museum of Art.

In any case, Glickman's musings were interrupted when an acquaintance approached him and invited him to have a drink across the street at the Café Select. He accepted. There, the artist and his companion were joined by an unfamiliar group of Americans. Dressed in unfashionably straight-laced clothing, the strangers espoused political beliefs that were highly disagreeable to Glickman. After hours of hotly contested debate, the artist decided to pay his part of the bill and go home, but one of the strangers—a man with a clubfoot—insisted on buying him a drink as a way to make up for their argument.

Instead of calling over the waiter who'd been serving drinks to the party all evening, the clubfooted man went to the bar himself and bought a Chartreuse for Glickman.

Before he even finished his cocktail, Glickman began to feel "funny." The walls appeared to move, the electric lights in the café were ringed with halos, and wine bottles seemed to levitate on Glickman's silent behest. Another member of the party told Glickman that he was now capable of "performing miracles."

Unbeknownst to Glickman, the clubfooted man had spiked his drink with LSD. The aftereffects of the acid trip sent him into a lifelong tailspin of psychosis, electroshock therapy, and terrifying hallucinations. He had no idea what had happened to him—this was 1952, at least a decade before most people had even heard of the drug. His social life was destroyed. He never had another romantic relationship (he told his Canadian girlfriend to leave him before he ruined her life). He took on a series of odd jobs, including cleaning furniture at a second-hand store. Glickman, who once had a promising future in the arts, never painted again.

Who was the mysterious poisoner? In all likelihood, it was Sidney Gottlieb, a man who dosed many other unsuspecting people with powerful hallucinogenic drugs during the 1950s. Infiltrating the seedier neighborhoods of San Francisco and New York, he poisoned prostitutes and their customers just to see what would happen.

The authorities were aware of Gottlieb's activities but did nothing to stop him. That may seem strange, until you learn that the man was an authority himself. For 22 years, Dr. Sidney Gottlieb ran the technical services division of the CIA and oversaw the CIA's MK-ULTRA program, an illegal drug and mind-control campaign launched during the height of Cold War paranoia. In addition to developing poison darts and toxic handkerchiefs for assassinating leaders of Communist governments, Dr. Gottlieb ran clandestine drug experiments on unsuspecting U.S. citizens. (It's not known exactly how many people were dosed, because in 1973 the director of the CIA, Richard Helms, ordered almost all records pertaining to MK-ULTRA to be destroyed.)

Gottlieb typically selected prisoners, poor people, petty criminals, and the mentally ill for his test subjects, since they were the least likely to be taken seriously should they have the temerity to complain about being drugged without their knowledge or consent by an upper-echelon federal official. (In all fairness, Gottlieb also enjoyed slipping mind-altering drugs into the drinks of his fellow CIA cronies, just for grins.) MK-ULTRA also ran tests on "willing" volunteers, like the seven people in Kentucky who were given LSD for 77 days in a row.

It's not known how many lives were ruined as a result of Gottlieb's hallucinogenic high jinks, but there's at least one documented case of a death resulting from his experiments. In 1953, at a U.S. Army research retreat at the Deep Creek Lodge in western Maryland, Gottlieb spiked after-dinner drinks with LSD without letting his fellow diners in on the joke. Frank Olson, a 43-year-old germ warfare researcher, became very disturbed by the experience. When he returned home, his wife and three children could hardly recognize the formerly jovial husband and father. They didn't have much of a chance to get to know this chemically transformed man, because nine days later, he jumped to his death from a 13-story window.

While some might call this murder, you have to remember that Dr. Gottlieb was acting in the interest of national security. In fact, during the 1977 Senate hearing on CIA abuses, Gottlieb told the committee that dosing unsuspecting human guinea pigs with drugs was justified. "Harsh as it may sound in retrospect," he testified, "it was felt that in an issue where national survival might be concerned, such a procedure and such a risk was a reasonable one to take."

Give credit to Gottlieb for being smart enough to work for an organization that would not only allow him to poison and murder people with such aplomb, but would also protect him from the consequences awaiting any other sociopath. Olson's widow fought years of heartrending legal battles until Congress agreed to award her $750,000 in exchange for releasing the CIA from liability. Glickman never received compensation for his unwilling role as a drug test subject. In fact, after he died in 1992, his sister sued the government. Despite the evidence against Gottlieb, the jury ruled against her. As for Gottlieb, he enjoyed his final years indulging his passions for folk dancing and goat breeding on his farm not far from CIA headquarters in Reston, Virginia. He died in 1999 at the age of 80. While his family refused to disclose the cause his death, it's not likely that *he* died as the result of a drug-induced suicidal jump from a hotel window.

MOST
APPALLING
CASE OF
EXTORTION

ORAL ROBERTS

I n the first half of the twentieth century, trucks carrying enormous tents crisscrossed the American Midwest. Pitched in dusty fields next to farming towns, the tents held thousands of people, often filled to capacity, with thousands more standing outside. All ears would be trained on the voice of the man onstage telling them how they could be cured of whatever ailed them through the power of God.

The most popular tent-show evangelist in the 1940s was an energetic young man from Pontotoc County, Oklahoma. Born in 1918 and prophetically christened Oral Roberts, the Pentecostal faith healer was a master with the microphone. Wiping the sweat of a hot summer evening from his face with a pocket handkerchief, Roberts dazzled Bible Belt crowds with his sizzling, high-speed oration and his astounding displays of "healing" the sick and crippled.

In 1949 Roberts started broadcasting a radio program, and by 1950 his 18,000-seat tent shows were played on 63 stations. In a few years, 400 radio and television stations were transmitting his show across the United States and Canada, and around the world via shortwave. By the 1960s, Oral Roberts's audience numbered in the millions. When the 1980s rolled around, evangelism had become big business, and Roberts had been joined on radio and television by a colorful cast of Christian characters: Jimmy Swaggart, Pat Robertson, Jerry Falwell, Robert Tilden, and Jim and Tammy Faye Bakker. Those whose ministries weren't derailed by sex scandals raked it in during those golden years. As long as they were able to keep their libidos under control, televangelists could get away with practically anything.

And none of them were—or are—more outrageous than Dr. Oral Roberts. He claims to have healed countless people afflicted with serious diseases, but his miracles are strictly limited to invisible, internal, or unverifiable maladies. People who hope Dr. Roberts will be able to regenerate a missing limb or make their skin cancer disappear are out of luck. (When his prayers failed to save his newborn grandson, he blamed it on the infant's "stubbornness.") Roberts also claims to have raised the dead, and says that when he dies, he'll rise again to co-rule the Earth with his partner, Jesus.

In September 1980, Oral Roberts said that a 900-foot apparition of Jesus met with him to discuss the completion of Dr. Roberts's City of Faith Medical and Research Center at Oral Roberts University in Tulsa, Oklahoma. Roberts recounted his meeting with the jumbo Jesus in a "Partner Letter" to his followers: "He stood a full 300 feet taller than the 600-foot-tall City of Faith. . . . He reached down, put his Hands under the City of Faith, lifted it, and said to me, 'See how easy it is for Me to lift it!'"

Roberts teaches his followers the doctrine of "Seed Faith," which holds that if you donate money (to Roberts) in the name of God, you'll get a manyfold return on your investment. And it works really well—for Roberts. His organization owns several luxury houses and he travels in a private jet.

Perhaps Roberts's most audacious stunt was his announcement that God had personally told him to raise $8 million for Oral Roberts University Medical School scholarships—or God would kill him. If that wasn't persuasive enough, Roberts's son, Richard, sent a threatening message to the flock: "IF YOU NEGLECT TO PAY ATTENTION. . .then Satan will take advantage and hit you with bad things and you'll wish 1985 had never come." Richard ended on an upbeat note, though, promising that any donation would "help get your hundred-fold return."

The press went ape over Roberts's threat, predicting that this latest stunt would end his career. But on April 1987, Roberts happily informed his followers that donations for the fund to keep God from snuffing him out totaled $9.1 million, over $1 million more than God had demanded.

A year later, the money was gone, and the 50 scholarship students at ORU were told that they'd each have to come up with $71,000 for tuition. Students who wanted to transfer to another college to avoid the fee were told they'd have to reimburse the cash value of scholarship money they'd already gotten plus 18 percent interest.

Money seems to go out as fast as it comes in, in Roberts's world. By September 1989, the 600-foot-tall City of Faith Medical and Research Center was bleeding money so fast that Roberts shut it down.

And still, people send him money.

WORST
MONUMENT
FOR FUTURE
GENERATIONS

**NUCLEAR WASTE
WARNING SYSTEM**

The world has generated an awful lot of radioactive waste in the last 60 years or so. The problem is, it will still be a problem after our generation is gone—*loong gone*. It's so dangerous, and there's so much of it, that it has ironically become a money-making "anti-commodity" on the world market. Russia is currently pursuing a plan that would make it the processor and repository for up to 21,000 tons of other countries' nuclear waste over the next decade, taking advantage of its nuclear facilities and abundance of remote dumping locations to earn an estimated $20 billion.

For its part, Russia's former Cold War rival, the United States has selected two sites to entomb its own spent nuclear reactor fuel rods and other detritus of the atomic age. One is Nevada's Yucca Mountain, and the other is New Mexico's Waste Isolation Pilot Plant. The U.S. Environmental Protection Agency has mandated that the waste destined for these sites be kept safe from the possibility of exposure for 10,000 years.

That's a tall order, but it's not even enough—the kind of radioactive material being stored will remain extremely lethal for at least 100,000 years. The EPA's plan is akin to sending a scuba diver on an hour-long mission with six minutes of air in the tank.

But ignore for a moment this literally fatal flaw and consider the enormity of the task at hand—how do you warn people from 10,000 years in the future to steer clear of these deadly dumps? After all, Stonehenge is only about 3,500 years old and experts can't figure out whether it's a big sundial or a monument to the vagina. Even now, it's difficult for most English speakers to comprehend Shakespeare without assis tance. And whatever language people from the year 12,000 will be speaking, it's not likely to be English.

In 1991 the Department of Energy, which manages nuclear energy in the United States, commissioned an anthropologist, an architect, a materials scientist, an astronomer, a linguist, and an archeologist to brainstorm on ways to create landmarks to warn people to stay away from the lethal waste.

Michael Brill, the architect on the team, wrote a paper about the experience entitled "An Architecture of Peril." He described the different messages that the landmarks were intended to convey to future generations. Among them: "This is not a place of honor . . . no highly esteemed deed is com-memorated here . . . nothing is valued here. What is here was dangerous and repulsive to us." He wrote that he and his fel-low experts decided that the "craftsmanship should be of low quality," and even though the "enormous size of the enterprise and of the structure demonstrates an enormous investment of labor . . . this coupling of great effort with material of low value suggests place is important but dishonored."

Some team members suggested a simple sign reading: DANGER: POISONOUS RADIOACTIVE WASTE BURIED HERE. DO NOT DIG UNTIL A.D. 12,000. This message would be repeated in every major language. The stone material into which these messages would be inscribed would have a lot of extra room to accommodate new languages as they arose. The words would be accompanied by bas-reliefs of a screaming face and a sick face. Others thought it would be unlikely that any language would survive that long and came up with a wordless comic strip that showed people running away from the bad place.

The experts also offered suggestions for structural elements designed to discourage anyone from digging around the site. "The Forbidding Blocks" option consists of a field of giant boulders spaced too tightly to walk between. "The Landscape of Thorns" would feature 80-foot-tall black rock spikes erupting from the ground at irregular angles. "Menacing Earthworks" would erect a bunch of lightning-bolt-shaped formations radiating from a central point. "Black Hole" would create a big round patch with cracks in it, suggesting parched, unusable land. According to Brill, these test designs were supposed to convey the idea of "wounding of the body through dangerous emanations; keeping something buried that must not escape; and dead, poisoned, destroyed land."

The sketches of the test designs are eerie, but they also exhibit an undeniable allure. They are works of art, and are therefore tempting traps for the curious.

In 2002 the Desert Space Foundation held a competition for new ideas to mark Yucca Mountain. Again, most of the new designs seem more like lures than repellents. "Blatant and permanent markers will increase, not reduce the probability of inadvertent intrusion," wrote Martin Pasqualetti, a professor of geography, in his paper "Landscape Permanence and Nuclear Warnings."

In light of this, perhaps one of the 1991 team's rejected suggestions should be reconsidered: simply leave a small portion of the radioactive material aboveground, so that anyone who wanders near it dies on the spot. What better deterrent than a pile of grotesquely blistered corpses?

MOST
INFAMOUS
CON

SELLING THE EIFFEL TOWER (TWICE)

Charles Ponzi stands as the exemplar of con artists. That's too bad, because his con, admittedly effective while it lasted, was crude and unimaginative. It amounted to little more than taking money from suckers and promising to pay them back at a ludicrously high rate of interest. Ponzi simply paid off earlier "investors" with money he took from people buying into the con later. Such a scheme is bound for catastrophe in the long run because, like a chain letter, it requires an ever-growing pool of suckers to maintain itself. Fraud is an ugly business, and Ponzi was certainly guilty of ripping off a lot of people—about 40,000—to the tune of $140 million in today's money. But the most infamous con in history was perpetrated by Ponzi's contemporary, Victor Lustig. Born on January 4, 1890, Lustig traveled the world posing as a wealthy European count. By blithely flashing around large wads of cash, he was able to gain the trust of his marks, whom he'd drain through elaborate long-term con games involving several accomplices. He reached the height of his dishonest trade when he sold the Eiffel Tower, not once, but twice, to an unsuspecting victim. Here's how he did it.

Arriving in Paris in 1925, Lustig read a newspaper story about maintenance problems with the Eiffel Tower. It was 36 years old, having been erected as a temporary monument for the 1889 Paris Exposition, and was supposed to have been torn down in 1909. Now it was in sorry shape, and upkeep was costing the local government a fortune. The city was even considering tearing it down rather than pay for the yearly repairs. Although that seems preposterous today, many Parisians at the time thought the Eiffel Tower was a crass eyesore ruining the classic architecture of their beloved city.

Ever on the lookout for an opportunity to direct other people's money in his direction, Lustig hired an unscrupulous printer to make some counterfeit government stationery. He assumed the role of Paris's Deputy Director General of the Ministère de Postes et Télégraphes, and sent letters to five of Paris's largest scrap dealers, asking them to attend a secret meeting at the impressive Hôtel Crillon.

Lustig wined and dined the men, then explained that the city government intended to tear down the tower and sell it for scrap. He told them Paris was accepting bids for the tower and swore them to secrecy, explaining that the government didn't want news of the controversial decision to be leaked to the public until everything was put in place. A couple of days later, Lustig rented a limousine and chauffeured the men to the Eiffel Tower, to explain certain particulars. He did this in order to observe the dealers' behavior, so he could pick the most gullible sucker. He selected André Poisson, because he seemed to be the most insecure about his station in the Parisian business world.

When the bids came in, Lustig called Poisson for a meeting and told him that he had won the contract—on one condition. Lustig said something to the effect of: "You see, I am only a poor civil servant, and cannot afford the things I would like to provide for my family. Perhaps you understand . . ." Poisson understood. In addition to handing over a fat wad of cash for the tower scrap, Poisson gave Lustig a healthy bribe for the privilege of being conned out of a huge sum of money.

Lustig hightailed it to Austria and waited for the story to explode in *Le Monde*. But there wasn't a whisper of it in the news. Apparently, the insecure Poisson was so ashamed about being grifted, he didn't report it to the authorities. Heartened by his good fortune, Lustig returned to Paris and pulled the stunt a second time with a new group of scrap dealers. This time, however, the mark got suspicious and called the gendarmes. The story hit the press, and Lustig was barely able to evade arrest. He landed in the United States, where he executed a number of other cons, but none so devious as the Eiffel Tower swindle.

WORST PHONE SERVICE

IRIDIUM

When a group of Motorola engineers brainstormed the idea for a global satellite phone system in 1987, it seemed like a great idea. In retrospect, Motorola probably wishes a meteorite had fallen on the whole lot of them.

At the time, mobile phones were bulky and expensive. Coverage was spotty, and service charges ran about a dollar a minute. Motorola's system would consist of 66 satellites in low Earth orbit, providing 24-hour wireless phone service all over the planet. In theory, it seemed smart. Smart enough for Motorola to start a new company called Iridium, plow $2.5 billion into it, and entice other investors to kick in an additional $2.5 billion.

Iridium was a massive undertaking, requiring 12 years to get off the ground. In addition to the awesome technological challenges, the company had to coordinate its efforts with dozens of countries in order to set up ground-based operational centers around the world. Shortly before the service was switched on in 1999, ads for Iridium service promised subscribers the ability to talk "with anyone, anytime, virtually anywhere in the world."

Notice the word "virtually"? That single word was to foreshadow the downfall of the entire enterprise. Because an Iridium phone, which cost $3,000 and looked like something a construction worker would clip to a utility belt—perhaps to pound nails—was as useless as a child's toy inside buildings. After $5 billion in development, the satellite's signal was too weak to penetrate roofs. If you wanted to make a call, you'd have to stand outside and establish a "line of sight" connection to a satellite for the privilege of paying Iridium $7 a minute to use the service. No one knows for sure why Motorola continued its fool's errand after realizing the phones worked only outdoors, but they forged ahead anyway, hoping snazzy ad campaigns would convince global jet-setters that the phone was a must-have item.

But by the 1999 launch of the system, as Motorola was stubbornly throwing good money after bad, the phone industry had evolved considerably. Cell phones had become small, sleek gadgets, and per-minute rates had dropped significantly. Wireless carriers had entered into nationwide roaming agreements that made it easy to use their phones over large geographic areas. By comparison, the Iridium phone was a dinosaur. Despite an intensified advertising campaign, Iridium never got more than 55,000 subscribers, a far cry from the 1.6 million the company had projected for 2000. In fact, it wasn't even making enough money to service the interest on the project's debt.

A little over a year after its launch, Iridium went bankrupt. The entire company was put on the auction block, but there were no takers, so the company made plans to knock the satellites out of orbit and let them burn up on reentry into the atmosphere. In December 2000, shortly before that was scheduled to happen, Boeing and several other buyers snapped up Iridium for $25 million, just one half of 1 percent of the original cost.

The new Iridium charges about $1 per minute to make a call. But you still have to walk outside to use it.

LEAST
GENIAL
FISH

The relationship between humans and fish has never been particularly cordial. In fact, most human-fish interactions involve one trying to eat the other. So far, humans have been winning on that end. Commercial fishing operations have come close to wiping out the Chilean sea bass, the swordfish, the orange roughy, and the cod, along with many other species.

Perhaps the candirú can be viewed as the fish world's agent of revenge against the human race. This parasitic South American catfish, which resembles an eel, measures up to five inches in length and lives on the blood of fish and mammals. The candirú is relentless in its pursuit of nourishment. One scientist who was handling a live specimen was shocked to see it make a beeline for a cut on his hand. The fish immediately burrowed itself under the scientist's skin and began working its way toward an artery.

The really frightening part about the candirú, however, is its ability to swim up and lodge itself into a human penis. Once the candirú gets into the urethra, it locks into place with rows of clawlike spines, lest anyone try to interrupt it from feasting on its host's blood and tissue.

In October 1997, a South American urogenital surgeon removed a candirú from a 23-year-old resident of Itacoatiara, Brazil. The man had been standing in the Amazon River, peeing into the water, when a candirú swam up the urine stream and wriggled into his penis. He tried to grab the part that was dangling out of the end, but it was too slippery. In an instant, the entire fish was inside.

When the man sought medical help four days later, he was in severe pain. He had a fever, his scrotum was swollen, and his abdomen was extremely bloated from the retention of urine. The surgeon inserted a tube into the patient's urethra and, with an alligator clip attached to the end of the tube, removed the fish. By this time, the fish had died and was starting to decompose, so the grip of its barbs had relaxed and the doctor was able to pull it out without ripping the man's urethra. With the aid of a small video camera attached to a flexible tube, the surgeon discovered that the candirú had traveled all the way up the patient's urethra to the sphincter, then, finding its way blocked, turned and chewed its way into the patient's scrotum (hence the swelling). Fortunately, in a follow-up examination a year later, the patient showed no aftereffects. It's safe to assume, however, that he'll be peeing on dry land from now on.

WARNING:
DO NOT URINATE
NEAR CANDIRÚ!

FATTEST FAST-FOOD SANDWICH

HARDEE'S
MONSTER THICKBURGER

People are exercising more than ever but are rapidly getting fatter. That seems odd, because in the 1950s, most people didn't exercise. They drank milkshakes and ate hamburgers. Why weren't they blimps like us? Why is it that we spend our spare time burning calories at the gym, yet can't stop layers of adipose tissue from expanding around our bellies, butts, and thighs?

The answer: We eat like pigs, and our grandparents didn't. The original McDonald's hamburger had 9 grams of fat. It still does, but who, besides a two-year-old, eats a regular McDonald's hamburger anymore? To our twenty-first century eyes, a McDonald's hamburger looks like a poker chip. The problem is, thanks to relentless "supersizing" over the years, our appetites have grown considerably, but our metabolisms still think we're living in the Stone Age, when meals were few and far between.

It comes down to math: Jogging burns off about 1 gram of fat per minute. You can work off the fat in a McDonald's hamburger in nine minutes. But if you want to erase the effects of a Big Mac's 32 grams of fat, you'll have to pound the pavement for a half hour. And if you plan on eating a Burger King Double Whopper (without cheese) on your lunch hour, you'll have to wolf it down in three minutes and then jog the other 57 minutes to fully degrease.

But the Whopper has nothing on Hardee's Monster Thickburger, described by the fast food franchise as a "monument to decadence." The unholy concoction of two-thirds of a pound of beef, three slices of cheese, four pieces of bacon, mayonnaise, and butter, delivers 1,420 calories and 107 grams of fat. Add a large side of fries and you're looking at 135 grams of pure fat, more than twice the maximum recommended daily limit, in one convenient meal! Try running that off in your spare time.

The latest in a line of intestine-stunning Thickburgers, launched by the restaurant chain in January of 2003, it's also the last straw for some health advocates. "If the old Thickburger was 'food porn,' the new Monster Thickburger is the fast-food equivalent of a snuff movie," said a spokesperson for the Center for Science in the Public Interest.

If the Monster Thickburger sounds like just the meal for you, you may not have to go far to get one. There are currently about 2,000 Hardee's restaurants in 14 countries around the world, including North and Central America, Asia, and the Middle East.

WORST
CASE OF
SPECULATIVE
HYSTERIA

TULIPOMANIA

Anyone who invested in the technology stock CMGI in 2000, when it was selling for $160 a share, only to watch it flatline to $1 a share a few months later, will be happy to learn that throughout history, people have periodically gone mad with speculative fever, sometimes losing their life's savings as a result.

The most colorful case of market insanity is *tulipomania*, a condition that afflicted Dutch traders in the seventeenth century. The exact timeline of Holland's love-hate affair with tulips is somewhat murky, but some scholars believe the flowers were introduced into the country by a botanist named Carolus Clusius in 1559, who planted a patch of them at the University of Leiden to study them for medicinal purposes. As more bulbs made their way to the country from Turkey, they seized the Dutch imagination. Their color was more intense than other flowers available, and their beauty and rarity made them symbols of power and prestige for the aristocracy and aspiring middle class.

In the ensuing years, tulips grew into a national obsession, and people spent considerable sums to purchase bulbs for their gardens. By 1630 interest in "fancy" tulip bulbs, which sprouted multicolored flowers, kicked prices into high gear. Three years later, people were trading a few bulbs for entire estates. Bulbs began selling faster than they could be grown or imported, and a futures market sprouted up, with bulbs that neither the buyer nor the seller had ever seen being traded several times in the course of a day. By this time, few buyers even planted the bulbs anymore, as they were considered too valuable to put in the ground.

A historian at the time recorded the exchange of a single bulb of a popular species called the "viceroy" for "four fat oxen, eight fat sheep, a complete bed, a suit of clothes, a silver drinking cup, two tons of butter, [and] one thousand pounds of cheese," plus more than 100 gallons of wine and enormous quantities of wheat, rye, and beer, for a total value of about 2,500 florins. A single bulb of the most precious species, the "Semper Augustus," could fetch as much as 5,500 florins. One transaction, consisting of 40 bulbs, sold for 100,000 florins.

Prices continued to climb until one fateful day in 1637, when the winner of some bulbs at an auction woke up from the mass delusion and refused to pay. His decision was like a slap on the head to jittery tulip traders, who took this as the sign that the inevitable end had arrived. In the ensuing market meltdown, prices plummeted a hundredfold, and those left holding bulbs for which they traded the family farm were ruined.

Today, 25 fancy tulip bulbs can be purchased at garden stores for about the price of a six-pack of beer.

MOST
DANGEROUS
TOY

JARTS

What's the worst toy in the world? Could it be one of the many vomiting, pus-spewing, flatulent dolls found on toy store shelves? Maybe it's the Mad Scientist: Dissect-an-Alien, advertised as a fun way to "Yank Out Alien Organs Dripping in Glowing Alien Blood," or an Ertl Blurp Ball, a line of squeeze toys that forcefully barf up the partially digested contents of their stomachs ("They Retch It, You Catch It!").

As bad as those toys are, they're nothing compared to playthings that maim. In the days before anybody cared about consumer safety, kids felt the cruel sting of all kinds of mayhem-inducing toys. In the early 1960s, the Air Blaster popped many an eardrum when children held the muzzle of the high-pressure air gun against their friends' ears and pulled the trigger. And the dark nature of Cabbage Patch Dolls was revealed in

1996, when a battery-powered "Snacktime" model with an articulated jaw bit onto a lock of its young owner's hair. The doll methodically gnawed its way up to the screaming girl's scalp and had to be removed by paramedics.

The worst toy of all, however, is not just dangerous, but downright deadly. It's hard to believe that Jarts—foot-long steel darts with plastic fins—ever made it to market. Sold as a backyard summer game by Franklin Sports Industries in the 1970s, Jarts were responsible for at least three child impalement fatalities between 1978 and 1988, when they were finally banned from sale. Hospital emergency rooms received more than 6,700 lawn-dart casualties during the toy's 10-year reign of terror.

While lawn darts of all kinds have been banned in the United States and Canada, they're still available in many other countries. United Kingdom–based Crown Darts sells them in a smaller blunt-tipped form and will ship them anywhere in the world except the United States. The company's advertising material states: "It seems ironic that in the U.S., citizens can purchase a firearm in many shops, but cannot get hold of a simple garden game that provides a lot of sociable fun for many people." And bruised noggins for a few of them.

MOST
UNSTOPPABLE
WEED

The villain of several contemporary science fiction stories is a substance known as "gray goo," consisting of sub-microscopic machines that reproduce quickly and consume everything they come in contact with, until the entire planet has been converted to gray goo.

Gray goo doesn't exist in the real world (yet), but we have the next worst thing: *Salvinia molesta*, a South American water weed that is rapidly spreading across New Guinea, Australia, Mauritius, Africa, India, Sri Lanka, New Zealand, and the United States leaving a trail of ecological suffocation and death in its wake.

Salvinia molesta goes by many aliases, including African pyle, aquarium watermoss, kariba weed, koi kandy, water fern, and water velvet. As the most unstoppable weed, it has three things going for it: First, it's an extremely fast multiplier. In optimum conditions, it can double in size every two days. A single *S. molesta* plant, given enough room to grow and sufficient sunlight, will spawn 67 million descendents in two months.

Second, *S. molesta* grows in floating, life-choking mats. A single mat can measure several feet thick and cover 60 thousand acres. These mats block sunlight and oxygen, killing the plants and animals that live below. It also gums up electrical generating systems and clogs irrigation conduits.

Third, it's almost impossible to kill *S. molesta*. When a boat propeller chops the plants into little pieces, each fragment regenerates into a new plant. In Hawaii, where the weed is causing serious damage to freshwater ponds, the government is using giant cranes to scoop it up and remove it (the weed weighs 36 tons per acre). The problem is that, unless every last plant is removed from a pond, the water will be covered again in a matter of months.

Is there any hope in sight? So far the answer seems to be no. As S. A. Abbasi, a professor of agriculture at Pondicherry University in India, writes in his book *Worst Weed (Salvinia): Its Impact and Utilization*, "Past attempts to control or destroy *Salvinia* by chemical or biological means have either been unsuccessful or have caused environmental backlashes, proving the cure to be worse than the disease." The book was published in 1993. Since then, *S. molesta* has continued to spread.

MOST
FLAGRANTLY
WASTEFUL
DOT-COM

PIXELON

The dot-com era of the late 1990s and early 2000s will be remembered by future generations as a period of mass foolishness driven by unbridled greed. How else will they be able to explain why companies with business plans for overnight delivery of 10-pound bags of cat litter could have valuations exceeding that of General Motors? Or how cash-losing propositions like Flake.com (a portal for breakfast cereals) could ever have received funding from venture capitalists in the first place?

The list of dot-coms that imploded after it became clear they were bleeding cash with no way to earn it back is endless, but one company, Pixelon, aptly encapsulates all that was wasteful and willfully stupid about the first Internet boom. Founded by Michael Fenne in 1996, Pixelon was touted to have technology that would make it possible to stream full-screen video over the Internet. Fenne convinced investors to fork over $23 million to market his technology, which he claimed to have developed while living in his automobile.

Some of Pixelon's investors may have been concerned when they learned of the company's Las Vegas launch party. For one thing, it cost $16 million, and featured performances by The Who, Kiss, the Dixie Chicks, Brian Setzer, Tony Bennett, Natalie Cole, and Faith Hill. For another thing, Web surfers who tried to watch the performances on their PCs using

Pixelon's technology reported that the software didn't work. But this was the 1990s—you had to spend a lot of money to get noticed, and this whole Web thing was new. Pixelon just needed to get the bugs out, that's all.

It's safe to assume that Pixelon's investors had more difficulty rationalizing the news that Fenne was not only a convicted embezzler, but was also one of Virginia's most-wanted bail-skippers. His name wasn't even Michael Fenne, it was David Stanley—and he was supposed to be serving an eight-year prison sentence for cheating clients out of more than $1 million.

Any Pixelon investors still clinging to the threadbare hope that they might get a return on their investment finally let go when told that Pixelon had been using a disguised version of a Microsoft application because its own technology didn't work. By May 2000, with Stanley now safely behind bars, the company went bankrupt.

WORST
INSECT
PEST

Meet the Formosan termite. She and her colony of five million sisters would like to visit your house. No need to invite her over, she can find her own way. Don't want her? Too bad—she'll chew through cement, utility poles, traffic light switch-boxes, plastic plumbing, phone cables, and bricks to get there. If you live in Japan, Guam, South Africa, Sri Lanka, Hawaii, or the southeastern United States along the Gulf of Mexico, she could be in your house already, but by the time you find out, it'll be too late to do much about it. She'll have reduced your house's structural interior to powder.

No homeowner likes termites, but of the 2,400 known species, only the Formosan triggers a heart-thumping panic. A colony can destroy a house in just a couple of years. Bug for bug, a Formosan termite eats wood nine times faster than other kinds of termites. A single Formosan colony has 10 times the members of other colonies, and unlike most other species, which limit their diets to dead and processed wood, Formosans happily devour *live* trees, plants, and crops—anything that has even a hint of wood in it.

Traveling from its native China to Taiwan (formerly Formosa, where the termite derives its name) to Japan, the pest has spread via lumber ships and other vessels to other parts of the world, most notably Louisiana. As soon as the six-legged immigrants hit the Port of New Orleans after WWII, their queens got busy, pumping out 2,000 eggs a day each. Today, a teeming network of untold billions of the translucent wood chompers live a couple of feet below the Big Easy, gorging on a half billion dollars' worth of property annually, much of it in the French Quarter historic district. Over 30 percent of the trees in New Orleans are infested, and falling trees damage numerous cars and buildings every year.

Despite attempts to stop them, Formosan termites continue to march across continents, hitch rides on ships across oceans, and leave trails of masticated sawdust behind them. Put out the welcome mat, you've got company coming.

WORST TENNIS DAD

CHRISTOPHE FAUVIAU

It's understandable that parents want their children to do well in sports. After all, most sports are healthful activities that can build confidence, coordination, and self-esteem, translating into success in other areas of life. Some parents, though, have a little too much sense of their own self-worth invested in their children's athletic accomplishments. It's embarrassing to witness a father screaming obscenities at a referee or umpire or, worse still, at other children. In extreme cases, parents go the extra mile and commit felonies in order to give their kids more than a sporting chance.

Some sort of parental anti-achievement award ought to be bestowed upon Wanda Holloway, the Texas mom who in 1991 wanted so badly for her daughter to win a spot on the cheerleading squad that she tried getting a hit man to rub out her daughter's 13-year-old rival as well as the girl's mother. Holloway served only six months in prison for her plot, which, fortunately, failed.

But the Ungrand Slam award surely goes to tennis dad Christophe Fauviau from Tercis-les-Bains, France, who is looking at a much longer stint behind bars for his attempt to ensure his children would sip from the winner's cup. In 2003 Fauviau's daughter was the number one 13-year-old tennis player in France, well on her way to a brilliant career, and her

16-year-old brother was a contender as well—but their dad wasn't taking any chances.

Unlike Holloway, Fauviau kept it simple, employing the quietly reliable assistance of Temesta, a drug prescribed for antianxiety that has a side effect of drowsiness. French authorities contend that Fauviau sneaked into the locker rooms of as many as 30 of his children's opponents and slipped a dose of the drug into their water bottles. (*Le Parisien* reported that Fauviau admitted to drugging his son's opponents but not his daughter's, a claim that investigators dispute.)

The plan worked, at least for a while. Many of the players complained of fatigue after losing a match to one of the Fauviau children. Papa was proud. But his children's tennis-playing futures came to a screeching halt on July 16, 2003. That was the day Alexandre Lagardère, a 25-year-old schoolteacher, dropped out of a match with Fauviau's son after just one set, complaining that he felt tired. While driving home after the aborted match, Lagardère fell asleep at the wheel and died when his car crashed. As it happened, the previous day another opponent of the son's saw Fauviau putting something into his water bottle. The boy, who didn't drink from his bottle but lost the match anyway, took it to the police, who analyzed it and found it had been laced with Temesta.

The police put two and two together, and Fauviau faces 20 years in prison if convicted of the charge of "administering a harmful substance and unintentionally causing the death" of Lagardère. As for Fauviau's daughter, it's likely her stellar tennis career ended at age 13, thanks to her father's murderous meddling.

MOST
INSENSITIVE
9/11
COMMEMORATIVE
SOUVENIR

Few people see the positive side to a disaster, especially one that causes the death of innocent people. But you have to wonder if a frisson of impending good fortune runs through the spines of memorabilia merchants when they learn of a major tragedy. To these sellers of plates, plaques, caps, and miniatures, disasters represent new profit opportunities.

Minutes after the *Columbia* space shuttle exploded on February 1, 2003, killing everyone on board, greedy eBay profiteers began selling souvenirs that ostensibly paid tribute to the fallen astronauts. In the weeks that followed, the Internet auction site was flooded with *Columbia*-related medallions, models, posters, patches, belt buckles, and a *"Columbia* Shuttle Tribute Bear"—a plush teddy bear with the vessel number embroidered on the soles of its hind paws and a hang tag printed with Psalm 57:10: "For great is your love, reaching to the heavens; your faithfulness reaches to the skies."

While all of this is appallingly tacky and heartless, it is nothing compared to the cavalcade of reverent trinkets arriving in the wake of the terrible events of September 11, 2001. Almost anything with a surface suitable for engraving or printing became fair game for profiteers of catastrophe—candleholders, throw rugs, Christmas tree ornaments, poker chips, silver ingots, replica firefighter helmets, handguns, serving trays, and bingo cushions.

Advertising come-ons for the items include such questionable platitudes as, "What better way to commemorate our nation's spirit and to mark a patriotic event that will continue to give Americans a feeling of hope and pride. Buy it today!"

Imagine torch lighters honoring the people who died in the Twin Tower infernos—someone has, and they're selling them with a straight face.

But the most thoughtless 9/11 souvenirs are the dozens of commemorative *knives* with images of the World Trade Center, weeping bald eagles, or quotes from President George W. Bush on them. Knives, the likely weapon of the hijackers themselves. Why not sell commemorative box cutters? Little canisters of commemorative jet fuel? If these guys had been around in the 1960s, you can be sure they would have sold replicas of Lee Harvey Oswald's bolt-action Mannlicher-Carcano rifle with an engraving of JFK on the stock.

MOST
APPALLING
ANIMAL
EXTINCTION

PASSENGER PIGEON

During the early nineteenth century in the eastern part of North America, it wasn't uncommon to witness a flock of passenger pigeons 300 miles long and a mile wide. The migrating birds would literally darken the sky, clouding the sun for the better part of a day. When landing to breed, a single colony could occupy 30 square miles of forest.

With a peak population somewhere between three and five billion birds by the time Europeans discovered America, passenger pigeons are thought to have been the most numerous bird on the planet. There were more passenger pigeons than birds of all other species in North America put together. As European immigrants cleared more and more forestland for settlements, the birds packed into the remaining forests, occasionally wreaking havoc on farmland (where they were shot in droves). Despite the loss of habitat, the pigeon population remained high.

So it wasn't deforestation, but rather people's taste for passenger pigeon meat (apparently it was quite tasty) and moreover the sheer fun of killing the birds that erased this species from the face of the Earth. It was considered great sport to fire guns (including early versions of the machine gun) into massive flocks just to watch the birds drop out of the sky. Passenger pigeon shooting competitions were popular. Contestants would often kill thousands of birds apiece. Roosting birds were netted, knocked out of trees with sticks, or stunned from their nests by pots of burning sulfur situated below. In 1878 a massive roosting site in Michigan was cleared at a rate of about 50,000 birds a day, with the killing going on for almost five months straight.

In 1896, when the passenger pigeon population had dwindled to a single flock of a quarter million birds, people scratched their heads in amazement. "What happened to all the birds?" they wondered, tracking the barrels of their guns back and forth across the sky.

The advent of the telegraph sealed the fate of the scarlet-eyed bird. It was used in April 1896 to transmit the location and size of the last flock to a team of hunters, who arrived at the scene and made short work of the birds. Killing 200,000 and wounding another 40,000, the hunters managed to whittle the flock down to about 5,000 pigeons. The remaining birds were tracked down and killed wherever they could be found.

On March 24, 1900, in Pike County, Ohio, a 14-year-old farm boy named Press Clay Southworth was feeding the cows on his family's farm when he saw an unusual bird eating corn in the barnyard. Running into the house to get a shotgun from his mother, he returned to shoot the bird dead. When Press showed it to his parents, they recognized the once-populous creature as a passenger pigeon. The boy took the bird to a local taxidermist, who used black shoe buttons for the bird's eyes. Today, the stuffed pigeon, known as "Buttons," is kept at the Ohio Historical Society in Columbus. Buttons is believed to have been the last known passenger pigeon alive in the wild.

By 1909 only three passenger pigeons were left, two males and a female. The birds were kept safe at the Cincinnati Zoological Gardens, but attempts to breed them were unsuccessful. By 1910 the males had died, leaving only the female, who was named Martha after the wife of the first U.S. president. Martha held on for four more years, dying on September 1, 1914, of natural causes. She was 29 years old.

LAMEST FORMER DICTATOR

VALENTINE STRASSER

n most respects, Valentine Strasser resembles any 30-something slacker. A college dropout, he lives in his mother's basement, wears a backward baseball cap, drinks beer, and complains about life not being fair. Really, the only thing that separates Strasser from other layabouts is his résumé: in 1992, at the age of 25, he forcefully overthrew the government of Sierra Leone, making him the youngest dictator in the world.

In 1991 Strasser was a captain in the Sierra Leone army. The country's leader, a military dictator named Major General Joseph Momoh, had not paid his soldiers in several months, so Captain Strasser and a group of fellow soldiers stormed the capital to stage a protest. It escalated into a full-blown coup, and on April 29, Captain Strasser found himself running the country.

While in charge of the impoverished African nation—which has a 74 percent illiteracy rate, a per-capita GNP of $160, and an average life expectancy of 37 years—Strasser did nothing to improve his citizens' lives. Rather, he just became another military dictator, filling the role with a seeming relish for clichés: He anointed himself with a silly title—Chairman of the Supreme Council of State and Head of the National Provisional Ruling Council. He talked a good game about being a champion of the people while looting the treasury. He flew to Antwerp with a suitcase filled with diamonds extracted from

Sierra Leone mines, in order to trade them for arms. He instituted a comprehensive torture program and drafted 12-year-olds into the army.

An Amnesty International Index report from 2001 reported that under Strasser's rule, "government forces were responsible for extrajudicial killings, torture and ill-treatment of captured or suspected rebel forces. They were also implicated in serious abuses against civilians, including deliberate amputations of hands." Strasser also got a reputation for rounding up political dissidents on the beach and then shooting them. Eventually Britain, which had been supplying aid to Strasser's regime in the mistaken belief that he was better than his predecessor, realized its mistake and cut him off. In 1996 the handsome young autocrat—who had a penchant for designer threads and wraparound sunglasses—was ousted in another military coup (fortunately for him, a bloodless coup), making him the youngest ex-dictator in the world.

Finding himself suddenly out of work, he changed his first name to Reginald and scored a law scholarship at a university in England (courtesy of the United Nations, which seemed to think there was still hope for him). According to the *Guardian*, he dropped out after 18 months and took a job as a bouncer at a nightclub. Apparently that job didn't suit him, but when he tried to go on the dole, the British government sent him packing back to Sierra Leone's capital, Freetown, where he took up residence on his mother's couch.

In 2002 Strasser told an Associated Press reporter, "I'm basically living off my mother now. She's been very supportive. It has been tough. I'm unemployed, but I'm coping."

Isn't there a self-help program for former despots?

MOST
REGRETTABLE
RELEASE OF AN
AGGRESSIVE
SPECIES

KILLER BEES

n October 1995, 88-year-old Mary Williams was walking near her house in Apache Junction, Arizona, when a swarm of bees flew out of a 13-foot-tall hive and began stinging her. A neighbor found Williams covered with bees and called for help. A fire crew that rushed to the scene used foam from its extinguishers to kill the bees, but it was too late. Four days later, Willams died as the result of having been stung more than 1,000 times by the bees.

A "killer" bee doesn't look murderous. In fact, it's impossible to tell the difference between a killer bee and a domesticated honeybee unless you perform a DNA test, or know what to look for under a microscope. Of course, another way to find out if a bee is killer bee is by swatting at it as it flies by. If it's an ordinary honeybee, it will most likely fly away. But a killer bee isn't so forgiving. It will become furious if you so much as stand near its colony. And it will stay mad for up to five days.

Killer bees are 10 times more likely to sting you than a domesticated honeybee, and they will chase you for a quarter mile to teach you a lesson. When agitated, a killer bee sends a signal to its pals, and in a matter of seconds you'll find yourself fleeing from a buzzing swarm of frenzied suicidal killers. Since arriving in the Americas in 1956, killer bees have stung to death around 1,000 people (not to mention 100,000 cattle). The sting of 300 bees is enough to kill a person, but swarms of killer bees have been known to strike a single victim with *8,000* stings.

How did killer bees get from Africa (their country of origin) to North America? Like a host of other unwelcome creatures— such as rats, garden snails, and pine beetles—people brought them over. In the case of the killer bee, the blame rests solely on the shoulders of one man, an eminent Brazilian geneticist by the name of Warwick Estevan Kerr. In 1956 Dr. Kerr imported several colonies of killer bees from Africa to South America because he was interested in crossbreeding them with European honeybees, to find out if the hybrid species would produce more honey.

He promised the Brazilian government that he wouldn't let a single bee escape. Less than a year later, a beekeeper accidentally let 26 killer bee queens loose from Dr. Kerr's experimental apiary outside São Paulo. Since then, the so-called Africanized honeybees have been stinging their way northward at a rate of between 100 and 200 miles a year, establishing new colonies and leaving swollen corpses in their wake.

The kicker? An Africanized honeybee colony produces one-fifth the honey of a European bee colony. Thanks a lot, Dr. Kerr!

SOUREST AUTO-MOTIVE LEMON

TRABANT SPUTNIK

It's hard to believe that any car could be worse than the Yugo—the shoddy Fiat knockoff made in the former Yugoslavia starting in 1954. Known as the Zastava in Europe, the cheap car was built for sale in eastern European countries, where most car buyers couldn't afford a real Fiat. Western Europeans wanted nothing to do with the jerry-built Zastava, and most Americans didn't even know the car existed.

Then, in 1986, an entrepreneur named Malcolm Bricklin took advantage of their ignorance and launched a massive campaign to import the car to the United States. It had a sticker price of just $3,990—thousands of dollars less than any other car on the market—and was promoted by snazzy commercials (one featured a parade of Yugos performing fancy synchronized weaves and zigzags across a blacktop). Yugo fever was in the air—buyers put down deposits on the cars sight-unseen, and dealer waiting lists ran five deep for every car to be delivered.

But when "lucky" new Yugo owners drove off the lot, they soon realized they'd been saddled with one of the sourest Serbo-Croatian lemons ever manufactured. Complaints poured in for sloppy assembly, low-quality materials, faulty brakes, premature rust, shorted electrical systems, broken transmissions, and engine failure. Yugo became the standard butt of car jokes (Q: How can you get a Yugo to do 60 miles per hour? A: Push it off a cliff.), and few shed tears when the Yugo manufacturing plant was destroyed in a 1999 NATO bombing raid. (The plant was also manufacturing munitions at the time, though many Yugo owners will insist the factory had been making bombs all along.)

As inconceivable as it might seem, there is a car even worse than the Yugo. Produced in East Germany under the directive of the Socialist government especially for the local market, the Trabant Sputnik was the epitome of Eastern bloc arrogance on four wheels. Steel was in extremely short supply in East Germany at the time (1957), forcing the Trabant's engineers to search for a substitute. Working with the materials at hand, they came up with a miracle substance they called Duroplast—made from wood pulp, sheep's wool, and tree sap—which was molded into cardboard panels to form the body of the car.

Beneath the car's surface, things were even worse. The engine, a tiny two-stroke model similar to a moped engine, made up for its pitiful weakness by spewing such an astounding quantity of foul-smelling exhaust that West Germany forbade ownership of the Trabant, and when *Car and Driver* magazine imported one into the United States to test it, the Environmental Protection Agency wouldn't let them operate it on public streets.

When the Trabant was first unleashed, everyone in East Germany wanted one—which isn't surprising, considering that the only other readily available modes of transportation were livestock and unwieldy bicycles. Unless you had a friend high up in the government, your name went last on a years-long waiting list. The most popular Trabant model, the P-601, was introduced in 1964. Free of troublesome valves, timing belts, oil pumps, water pumps, crankshafts, and many other items found in most cars, the P-601 remained essentially unchanged for three decades.

With the fall of the Berlin Wall, however, East German residents fled from their reviled "Trabis" like they were on fire, buying used Volkswagens and other cars made in the free world. The Trabant company attempted to compete by making knockoffs of real cars, but by 1990, the Trabi era had come to a close.

Today most people would like to forget the Trabant, but that's hard to do. Unlike steel, Duroplast is nonrecyclable, and the carcasses of unwanted Trabis litter the German countryside, serving as unfond reminders of the days when the worst car ever built ruled the roads of one of the worst countries ever established in the twentieth century.

MOST
DISINGENUOUS
BUTCHER

FRITZ HAARMANN

Life in post-WWI Germany wasn't pleasant. The economy was in shambles, work was scarce, and healthy food was hard to come by. So the residents of Hannover were happy when in 1918 a petty thief named Fritz Haarmann started selling choice cuts of pork on the black market. Where did he get it? Well, it was meat, it was fresh and tasty, and it was plentiful, so nobody asked the question out loud. Why ruin a good thing? The police didn't bother Haarmann, either, because he was a valuable informant for the department, eager to turn in fellow criminals for a small sum.

But in 1924, when a boy last seen with Haarmann was reported missing, the police felt it their duty to visit the jovial black-market butcher. Upon searching his apartment, they discovered piles of bloodstained clothing on the floor. A search of a nearby river dredged up the remains of 23 young men. Haarmann was arrested for the murders but was offended by the charges, claiming he had killed far more than 23. By his estimate, he'd murdered about 40 young men, near the end of his run offing about 2 a month.

His favorite trick was to impersonate a police officer, round up young men in public lavatories, then bring them to his filthy apartment where he'd molest them. Then, as he told the court, "I would throw myself on top of those boys and bite through the Adam's apple, throttling them at the same time." After disposing of the identifiable body parts, he'd butcher the boys into chops and take them to market, where customers would unwittingly purchase the human meat. It was a win-win situation for Haarmann: not only was he well-compensated for killing his victims, but his customers ate the evidence.

Dubbed by German newspapers the "Hannover Vampire," Haarmann was beheaded on December 20, 1924.

WORST HYPER-INFLATION

When a government runs out of money, often the first thing it will do is raise taxes. But in circumstances of severe economic depression, if there isn't much money to go around, this may not kick up enough cash. The government must then try to borrow funds to make ends meet, but most investors will avoid that risky proposition. A third option—invading another country to seize its wealth—is generally frowned upon by the international community and destined to fail unless the government is rich enough to finance the operation. That leaves one other choice: crank up the knob on the treasury printing press and hope nobody will notice.

Unfortunately, this last trick makes about as much sense as topping off a bottle of vodka with tap water. It might look full, but you'll have to drink more of it each time you want to get drunk. Eventually, the vodka becomes zero proof and the charade ends.

The most famous instance of this kind of hyperinflation took place in post–World War I Germany. The German government was in deep trouble, and it decided to buy its way out by printing money with nothing to back it up in its federal reserves. In short order, the economy was flooded with currency, and prices rose accordingly. In order to pay the higher prices, the government printed even more money, and prices shot up even more. In the period between August 1922 and November 1923, prices increased a trillion percent. The exchange rate in 1923 was 4 trillion marks per U.S. dollar. Germans ran through the streets with wheelbarrows of cash in hopes of buying a bag of salt from anyone foolish enough to sell it. Life savings were wiped out, businesses were ruined, and the economy imploded.

But as bad as Germany's inflation was in the 1920s, it was nothing compared to the hyperinflation that occurred as a result of the civil war in Yugoslavia. In 1990, following the end of Communist rule, a new dinara was issued, equal to 10,000 of the old dinaras. But inflation continued to climb, especially after Yugoslavia was hit by an international embargo. To finance its war effort, the government issued yet another dinara in 1993, equal to 10 of the previous dinaras. New dinaras continued to replace previous dinaras on a regular basis. The 1994 dinara was worth one billion previous dinaras.

Needless to say, these moves had little effect on stabilizing the economy—after all, who trusts a 500,000,000,000-dinara bill? By that time, 100,000,000,000,000,000,000 (100 quintillion) 1994 dinaras had the purchasing power of a single 1989 dinara and the populace had given up using them, turning instead to barter and currency from other countries. Ironically, the Yugoslav government successfully stabilized the dinara in 1994 by tying it to the German mark, the classic symbol of hyperinflation.

MOST
UNAPPEALING
FETISH

Anyone with an Internet search engine can find videos and pictures online to fulfill any fetish—from fantasies about being eaten alive by giant women to placing saddles on ordinary-sized women and riding them in circles around the living room. If you can think of it, it's probably out there. Most fetish videos are perfectly legal, and because they often have no nudity or profanity in them, they could conceivably be sold to children.

But the freewheeling fun grinds to a halt when a fetish involves the destruction of bugs and small animals. Called "crush videos," they depict insects, hamsters, and other little creatures being squashed and killed under the feet of fully clothed women. The Society for Animal Protective Legislation estimates that there are 2,000 animal snuff videos in print, with titles such as *Vanessa's Frog Stomp* (featuring more than 100 tree frogs getting squashed under a woman's high-heeled sandals), *Mistress Di, Princess of Death* (who squeezes mice to death by placing them between sheets of Plexiglas and sitting on them), and *The "Tails" of Charlie's Ankles* (in which a woman tells a mouse squirming under her foot, "You're going to listen, and you're going to die my way," before crushing the mouse's head under her high-heeled shoes).

The women's faces are rarely shown in crush videos— the camera focuses on their feet and the animals' horrifying deaths (according to psychologists who have studied the fetish, crush videos appeal to patrons who identify with the animals being tortured). High-quality microphones are used to pick up the sounds of the rodents' squeals and their bones snapping. While most crush videos feature small animals, some use cats, dogs, and monkeys.

In the United States, the foot came down on crush videos in 1999, when President Clinton signed a law prohibiting their possession and distribution, but they are still available from Web sites in countries that don't have laws against them. According to the SAPL, they are particularly popular in the United States, Brazil, Dubai, Japan, Mexico, and across Europe.

MOST
UNWANTED
GARBAGE

CARGO OF THE *KHIAN SEA*

Almost by definition, garbage is stuff nobody wants. You usually have to pay someone to take it off your hands. Sometimes, if the garbage is *really* unwelcome or it just has nowhere to go, a company will pay another country to accept it. That was the case with the trash aboard the *Khian Sea*, a 466-foot garbage barge owned by Joseph Paolino and Sons.

On September 5, 1986, it left Philadelphia, carrying 14,855 tons of incinerated household garbage (essentially just ash). The city, desperately short of landfill space, had earlier tried to get rid of the garbage by paying neighboring states to take it, but they were facing their own landfill crises. So the barge headed for a manmade island in the Bahamas owned by the Amalgamated Shipping Company, which had agreed to take the garbage. On its way to the islands, however, the

Bahamian government got wind of the deal and refused to give the barge permission to dock. Forced to turn back, the barge tried to unload the ash in Bermuda, Puerto Rico, the Dominican Republic, Honduras, and the Netherlands Antilles. But everyone was suspicious of the garbage, figuring it had to be highly toxic.

In 1987 the *Khian Sea* managed to dump 4,000 tons of it on a beach in Haiti, telling the government it was "fertilizer." The barge then headed east for Africa, trying to discharge the rest in Cape Verde, Guinea-Bissau, and Senegal. They wouldn't have it. Like the Little Engine That Could in the children's book, the barge puffed its way across the ocean to faraway ports in Borneo, Indonesia, the Philippines, and Sri Lanka. None of those countries wanted it, either. More than once, the barge was refused entry to a port at the barrel of the harbormaster's gun. Even renaming the barge the *Felicia* in the hopes of sneaking it into a port unnoticed didn't work. Neither did selling the barge to a new owner.

The thing that *did* work was dumping the remaining 10,000 or so tons of ash into the sea in November 1988 when no one was looking. When the barge arrived in Singapore empty, officials got suspicious. In 1993 two executives at the company that owned the barge were sent to prison for the stunt.

But that's not the end of the story. In 1996, responding to the outcry of environmentalists, the U.S. government ordered the ash that had been unloaded in Haiti to be picked up. A new barge, the *Santa Lucia*, collected the ash in 2000 and docked in Martin County, Florida. Eastern Environmental Services, which was linked to the now-defunct Joseph Paolino and Sons and therefore responsible for the ash, tried to convince

Cherokee Nation in Oklahoma, and Broward County in Florida to take the stuff, but neither wanted it. Like everyone else, they thought it was contaminated.

In 2002 Glenn Henderson, a columnist for the *Palm Beach Post*, went aboard the barge to see what the ash looked liked. He reported: "Squeezing between multitudes of spider webs, I peered down into the 'hold' and couldn't believe my eyes. Australian pines were everywhere, some as tall as 10 feet. There were dandelions, weeds with small blue-and-yellow blossoms, patches of seemingly manicured grass, and tall brown weeds resting in layers across grayish piles punctuated by pure-white chunks of who-knows-what. And there was a hibiscus plant with pretty pink blooms."

Soon after, the U.S. Department of Agriculture, U.S. Environmental Protection Agency, city of Philadelphia, Florida Department of Environmental Protection, and U.S. Biosystems all tested the ash and determined it to be nonhazardous. Finally, it was disposed of at the Mountain View Reclamation landfill in Franklin County, Pennsylvania, just miles from its point of departure 16 years earlier.

MOST
HORRIFIC
SELF-HELP
TECHNIQUE

Are you having more difficulty concentrating these days than in years past? Do you tire easily? Is your memory failing? Face it—you're getting older, and your brain isn't what it used to be. You could go to the doctor to see if there's a drug or vitamin supplement that could help. You could try various mental exercises to keep your mind stimulated. Or you could simply buy a drill and bore a hole in your head.

That's what 23-year-old Pete Halvorson of Wernersville, Pennsylvania, did on August 17, 1972. No, he wasn't trying to end it all. Quite the contrary—he was drilling for a new beginning. Halvorson is a proponent of trepanation, a medical procedure that was all the rage in medieval days, back when bloodletting and cauterization were the surefire cures for many ailments.

Halvorson became interested in trepanation after reading about its purported benefits in a 1962 book titled *Homo Sapiens Correctus: The Mechanism of Brainbloodvolume*, written by a Dutch medical student named Hugo Bart Huges. Huges claimed that drilling a small hole (between one-quarter and one-half inch in diameter) through the skull causes additional blood to flow through the brain's capillaries, resulting in increased mental abilities. ("I feel as I felt before the age of fourteen," Huges told an interviewer.)

Intrigued, Halvorson decided to undergo the procedure. After being turned down by several doctors who refused to make a hole through his head, Halvorson took matters into his own hands and pierced his skull with an electric drill. Now, over 30 years later, he says he has plenty of energy, can stay focused, and "feels good all the while."

Brain specialists say trepanation should stay in the Stone Age, where it originated. The Inca people of 6000 B.C. trepanned people as a way to let out demons trapped in their heads; in the Middle Ages, it was used a treatment for epilepsy. Unfortunately, 4 out of 10 epilepsy patients died from the infections that frequently followed trepanation. Today, doctors warn that the risk of brain injury, infection, and blood clots isn't worth the unproven benefits.

The International Trepanation Advocacy Group, directed by Halvorson, boasts 15 "volunteers"—people who have had the procedure in the interest of providing data to support the hypothesis that trepanation is beneficial. ITAG has yet to find a doctor in the United States or Europe willing to perform the surgery, but they've got one in Mexico lined up who, for about $2,500, will gladly drill a hole in your skull.

MOST
STUBBORN
SOLDIER

LIEUTENANT HIROO ONODA

When 23-year-old Japanese soldier Hiroo Onoda was sent to Lubang Island in the Philippines in December 1944, he took his orders very seriously. The division commander made it clear he didn't want Lieutenant Onoda to give up, telling him he wasn't allowed to lose the island to American forces, or even to kill himself, no matter how dire the circumstances. He also promised Onoda that he would return for him when it was time to come home.

Not long after the lieutenant began leading his guerilla fighters on the island, U.S. Marines arrived and killed or captured most of the Japanese soldiers. Onoda and three others managed to escape into the hilly jungle interior, where they holed up with little more than their rifles and a small supply of rice.

Weeks turned into months. When the rice ran out, Onoda and his men subsisted on bananas and coconuts. They also stole cows and other supplies from villages. In October 1945, the United States dropped leaflets on the island announcing that the war had ended in August and that any Japanese soldiers still in hiding could come out without fear of being harmed. But Onoda would not be fooled by the Americans' trickery. He ordered his men to stay put and keep their rifles clean.

When the Allies letter-bombed the island again—this time with copies of General Yamashita's surrender order—Onoda again saw through the ruse. The note stated that upon surrender, they'd be given "hygienic succor" and would be "hauled" back to Japan. Neither of these things sounded right to him. Nice try, G.I. Joe!

As the years went on, Onoda's family members came to the island with photographs and newspapers from Japan to prove that the war had ended. They pleaded on loudspeakers for weeks on end, begging him to come out and return home with them. Onoda was impressed by the Allied forces' excellent paper forgeries and voice impersonators, but in every instance, he was able to pick out a mistake or inconsistency that gave the trick away. Around this time, Onoda and his men began ambushing and sometimes killing local villagers, after he had determined that they were actually U.S. spies dressed as farmers.

By 1949 some of Onoda's men began to wonder if there might be more to life than eating bananas, shooting at farmers, and providing a food source for mosquitoes. One of the soldiers surrendered. In 1954 another was shot and killed while attacking villagers. Only Onoda and one other soldier remained.

For the next 18 years, the two men lived in the jungle, coming down to conduct the occasional surprise raid on villagers. Perhaps Onoda had mule blood coursing through his veins, because when his last soldier was killed in 1972, the 50-year-old lieutenant still stubbornly refused to call it quits.

Two years later, a young Japanese traveler named Norio Suzuki arrived in Lubang on the first leg of a mission to find three exotic and elusive creatures of the wild: a panda, a yeti, and Onoda. He somehow managed to meet Onoda, and, remarkably, gain his trust. (In his autobiography, *No Surrender*, Onoda says the fact that Suzuki wore sandals and thick wool socks was a dead giveaway that he was a true Japanese and not a spy.) Suzuki implored Onoda to come back to Japan with him, but Onoda said nothing doing. He would only answer to his commanding officer, Major Yoshimi Taniguchi.

Suzuki tracked down Taniguchi, now the owner of a bookstore in Osaka. On March 9, 1974, Suzuki and Taniguchi went to Lubang and met with Onoda, who stood at attention while Taniguchi ordered him to lay down his weapon and cease combat—nearly 30 years after the end of World War II.

Onoda unloaded the bullets from his perfectly maintained rifle and returned with the two men to a very different Japan, where he was hailed as a hero despite having killed 30 or more Filipinos and wounding at least 100 others. After receiving a pardon from Philippine president Ferdinand Marcos, Onoda moved to Brazil and bought a cattle ranch, and so far has kept his own herd away from any remaining WWII jungle holdouts who might be hungry for steak.

MOST
REPUGNANT
ADVERTISING
SCHEME

PIZZA HUT LOGO ON THE MOON

People like to stare at the moon. It elicits feelings of wonder and awe. Ten million years ago, our pre-human ancestors were probably just as entranced by its beauty and mystery as we are. It wasn't until 1998 that an advertising executive happened to look up at the ancient orb and think: "billboard."

That was the year Pizza Hut tried to put its logo on the moon. The company hired a team of experts from Washington's National Observatory, Hughes Space and Communications International, the Federal Aviation Administration, and New York's Hayden Planetarium to ask how it could be done. A plan emerged to use the moon as a backdrop for the logo as projected by a high-powered laser beam. The thinking seemed to be that people who saw the company's red roof and name logo imposed upon the moon's image would be so impressed that they'd order a pizza from or visit one of the global restaurant chain's more than 10,000 locations worldwide.

The scheme was foiled when the experts told Pizza Hut that the logo would have to be as big as the state of Texas to be seen from Earth, and laser technology was not up to such a Herculean task. A secondary concern was that such a system could blind airplane pilots flying at night.

Pizza Hut had to scrap its plans. But rest assured, when lasers are developed to sufficient strength, and the pesky blind-pilot problem solved, we may yet be lucky enough to live in a Dean Martin world where "the moon hits your eye like a big pizza pie."

Plan B, which went off without a hitch in 1999, had Pizza Hut pay the Russian government more than a million dollars to put a 30-foot-tall logo on the side of a Proton rocket, which was launched from Kazakhstan to carry a service module to the International Space Station. This was a bargain compared to the 1996 stunt pulled by Pizza Hut's parent company, PepsiCo., when it pumped $5 million into Russia's ailing space program to have Mir Space Station cosmonauts play with a giant-size inflatable Pepsi can in space. Now, this is money well spent. How often can you purchase cans of sugar to fund an experiment to see if serious scientists of a world super-power would be willing to demean themselves by behaving like circus clowns?

The WORLD'S BEST

A number of friends and colleagues assisted in the writing of this book. Thanks to the following people for suggestions and support: David Pescovitz, Kelly Sparks, Gareth Branwyn, Craig Shapiro, Elizabeth Kruger, and Nina Frauenfelder.

Special thanks to Alan Rapp at Chronicle for championing my proposal and offering initial guidance, and to my lovely wife Carla Sinclair, for going over every entry and weeding out anything that wasn't bad enough to make the cut.

How-can-I-ever-repay-you thanks to my editor, Steve Mockus, both for his mind, which is sharper than a mono-molecular obsidian blade edge, and for his dedication to the project, which was as relentless as a door-to-door magazine salesman under orders to meet quota. Thanks also to Brett MacFadden and Tera Killip for helping guide the book to fruition, and to Tim Belonax for the superb design job.

While I take complete credit for everyone's contributions, the blame for any errors must rest solely on their shoulders.

—Mark Frauenfelder

The WORLD'S WORST AUTHOR AND ILLUSTRATOR

Mark Frauenfelder is the editor-in-chief of *Make* magazine and the author and illustrator of *Mad Professor*. He has written for numerous publications, including the *New York Times, LA Weekly, Wired, Popular Science,* and *Playboy.* Co-founder of the popular Boing Boing weblog (www.boingboing.net), he lives in Southern California.